ZIPPERS, SNAPS, AND FLAPS

An Array of Fifty-four Easy-to-Make Toys

Phyllis Fiarotta and Noel Fiarotta

VNR **VAN NOSTRAND REINHOLD COMPANY**
New York   Cincinnati   Toronto   London   Melbourne

Copyright © 1983 by Van Nostrand Reinhold Co. Inc.
Library of Congress Catalog Card Number 82-15898
ISBN 0-442-22542-3

Printed in the United States of America
Designed by Rose Delia Vasquez

Published by Van Nostrand Reinhold Company Inc.
135 West 50th Street
New York, New York 10020

Van Nostrand Reinhold Publishers
1410 Birchmount Road
Scarborough, Ontario M1P 2E7, Canada

Van Nostrand Reinhold Australia Pty. Ltd.
480 Latrobe Street
Melbourne, Victoria 3000, Australia

Van Nostrand Reinhold Company Limited
Molly Millars Lane
Wokingham, Berkshire RG11 2PY, England

16 15 14 13 12 11 10 9 8 7 6 5 4 3 2 1

Library of Congress Cataloging in Publication Data
Fiarotta, Phyllis.
Zippers, snaps, and flaps.

Includes index.
Summary: Presents instructions for fifty-four toys to sew
with parts that can be zipped, pocketed, or snapped, such as
dollar bill containing coins that total one dollar.
1. Toy making.   [1. Toy making.   2. Sewing.
3. Handicraft]   I. Fiarotta, Noel.   II. Title.
TT174.F5   1983   745.592'4   82-15898
ISBN 0-442-22542-3

In loving memory of our fabulous mother who gave us a childhood filled to the brim with endless hours of magic and wonderment, and who continued to perpetuate it long after we grew up to be people.

Also to the memory of Bunny Williams, who, like our mother, never let the glitter of childhood escape from her heart.

Here's till we all meet again in that eternal toyland in the sky.

CONTENTS

Introduction

Little children, their bodies and minds yearning to develop, live in an environment filled with constant changes and continuous curiosities. Everything that appears before their wandering eyes is fair game for inquisitive touch and thorough investigation. As adults, we often wish juveniles would keep their hands at their sides, but the wonders of the world lie just beyond the grasp of tiny, analytical fingertips.

Being very young and small is a special season of life and truly an age bathed in softness. Children of preschool age and younger are afforded the Three S's—Softness, Smoothness, and Scent. All of the products geared for this age group are marinated in these qualities, and nary a rough edge, abrasive texture, nor caustic odor should ever be found. This is quite true of the toy industry, and in keeping with this tradition, all of the toys in this book are made of felt or fabric and are softer than a baby's "you know what."

The fifty-three projects you are about to discover are either derived from children's literature or taken from the experiences of everyday living. Some introduce educational concepts, while others provide pure enjoyment. A child can learn about the different coins that add up to a dollar, investigate which vegetables make a soup tasty, become an astronaut rocketing to Mars, learn all about the characters in the popular fairy tales, or snuggle in bed with The Owl and the Pussycat. All of the toys are designed so that individual parts are either zipped, tucked, or snapped into place. This unique feature will help little children develop better eye/hand coordination skills and will provide a sense of independence—with so many pieces with which to play comes the responsibility of putting them back where they belong, after playtime has ended. The toys are fun to hold and play with, so learning and discovering becomes delightful. There are also projects that complement the holidays, and involving your little ones in these special times benefits the entire family.

The book is designed and written so that the young child will enjoy flipping through the pages with his parent, perhaps picking out some favorite projects while the parent reads about them aloud. All the necessary pattern pieces are provided, along with complete, easy-to-follow directions. The materials needed are inexpensive and readily accessible, and all of the projects can be made with a needle and thread or some glue.

At one time, all toys were made by hand, but now, finding a toymaker is as rare as finding a three-dollar bill. You can keep this special craft alive by making one, some, or all of the toys in the book. Just think. Some day, while cleaning out a closet or the attic, your son or daughter will come across one of these toys. The first sentiment that will lovingly come to mind will be, "Gee, my mom made this for me."

Sewing Supplies

Zippers

Many projects in the book are designed so that individual parts are zipped into a bag that complements the toys. Although every bag is different in size and shape, each has a side that will accommodate a zipper. All of the zippers called for in the instructions are standard-size skirt zippers (with one open end) or dress zippers (with both ends closed). Either type works well. There are also many styles of fabric tape fasteners, packaged under numerous brand names, that can be good substitutions for zippers.

Snaps

Some projects in the book have individual parts that are snapped into place, such as the tea cups in Mother Hubbard's cupboard or the swinging arms on the Toy Soldier. Sewing snaps are available in several sizes, but the largest ones are the easiest for little hands to manipulate. In some cases, bits of tape fasteners, metal fasteners, and hooks and eyes can be used.

Felt

Felt is the primary material used in the book as it is nonwoven, sturdy, and does not require hemming. It can be bought in small rectangles in a wide variety of colors at most sewing counters. In larger sewing centers, felt is sold by the yard in several weights. If you have a choice, choose a sturdier weight. Save every scrap of felt in a plastic bag for use as small appliqués, facial features, and spot designs.

Fabric

Although a great number of the toys require felt, fabrics can be substituted for many of the individual dolls. Choose sturdy, washable fabrics. Since the edges of most fabrics will unravel and fray, read the sewing instructions in Sewing Procedures carefully.

Interfacings

There are many parts of the toys that need a layer of interfacing for extra body. In a few cases it is called for specifically in the instructions, but do not hesitate to use it where you think it necessary.

Stuffings

Most stuffings available today are nonallergenic polyester, packaged in large bags. They are lightweight and washable. Cotton fill is becoming harder to find and is not as versitile as polyester. When parts of a project require a slight stuffing, quilt batting, a large sheet of polyester that has been precut, works well.

Trims

Any toy in the book can have an extra bit of pizzazz with the addition of a decorative sewing lace, ribbon, trim, cord, sequins, or any other brightly colored bauble. Keep some on hand.

All About Patterns

The Grid

Have you ever enthusiastically attempted a craft project, but could not progress beyond drawing the design? "I can't draw a straight line" is a common excuse for shelving a worthwhile idea. Drawing a straight line is quite easy—it's the curved lines and the fine details that pose the most difficulty. One sure way to accurately reproduce or transfer designs is to use a grid, an important tool for craftspeople, neophytes and experts alike. To draw a grid, all you need is a straight edge and a drawing tool. But if you prefer to trace your grid, refer to the end of this book: there are grids in four often-called-for sizes (¼ inch, ½ inch, ¾ inch, and 1 inch) for your use.

There are two basic elements of a grid. The first is the boxed network of horizontal and vertical lines that form the grid, or graph. The second is the design or designs placed on it. Most projects in the book call for designs placed on grids. If you have never worked with a grid, the following information will be of value to you. Practice with any of the designs in the book.

Studying the Grid

The key to working with a grid is understanding the instructions that accompany it. If the scale of a grid is 1 square = 1 inch, each square of the final grid will measure exactly 1 square inch. Suppose a grid is 8 squares wide; the width of the completed design will measure 8 inches.

Drawing the Grid

To start the grid, draw the first horizontal line (left to right) close to the top of a sheet of paper. If the scale of the grid is 1 square = 1 inch, measure 1 inch below each end of the line, and make a mark. Connect both marks with a straightedge. Continue to plot 1-inch horizontal lines until you have matched the same amount of lines shown in the grid you are working with. Draw the first vertical line close to the left edge of the paper, perpendicular to the horizontal lines. Plot the vertical lines in the same manner as you did the horizontals. If a design calls for a scale of 1 square = 3 inches, for example, follow the same procedure as above but use a 3-inch measurement.

For your convenience, ¼, ½, ¾, and 1-inch "instant grids" are predrawn at the back of the book. Simply trace the grid you need onto tracing or tissue paper. If you need a grid to cover a larger area, trace the graph twice, side by side—or four times, to form a large rectangle.

Placing the Line Drawing

Placing a line drawing on the grid is just a matter of concentration. Study how lines pass from square to square. Do they cut corners, pass diagonally, or curlicue through the boxes? Recreate the exact path of each line as it moves from square to square.

Adjusting the Grid

Grids in the book are ¼, ½, ¾, and 1 inch. These scales are merely suggested sizes for individual projects. You can enlarge or decrease the size of any toy by making the grids larger or smaller. Do not forget to adjust the size of your zippers if you change the size of the pattern.

Choosing the Correct Paper

For small patterns, drawing paper or typing paper will suffice. For larger patterns, use brown wrapping paper or large brown supermarket bags. If you like working with lightweight paper, use tracing paper or giftwrap tissue paper.

What To Draw With

A pencil, of course, is the best drawing tool because it can be erased, but fine-tip markers—with or in place of a pencil—can also be quite successful. Draw your grid with a pencil or a light-color marker. Once you have drawn the design and made all necessary adjustments, draw over the lines with a red or other color marker for added clarity.

Cutting Out a Pattern

The rule of thumb when cutting out a pattern is to cut a little beyond the lines on the paper instead of following the outline directly. It is better to make patterns slightly larger than slightly smaller.

Traced Patterns

Many patterns here are drawn in their intended sizes. A pad of tracing paper, sold at variety or stationery stores, should be an ample supply of pattern paper.

Freehand Patterns

There are many instances when you can forgo the grid or traced pattern and draw designs freehand on paper or directly on the fabric. This is especially recommended for small details such as facial features.

Direct Patterns

If you have a keen eye, there are many simple designs in the book that can be cut out directly from fabric, without drawing or making a pattern. In these cases, specific measurements and cutting procedures are given.

Pinning Patterns

A large supply of straight pins is a must for anyone who sews. Heavy paper patterns tend to buckle slightly when pinned to fabric, so be sure to add enough pins to flatten them sufficiently. When cutting out fabric shapes, always cut a little away from the patterns, never into them.

About Metrics

All measurements here are given in inches and feet. For those of you who work in the metric system of measurement, here are the conversions you should use.

Linear Measure
1 inch = 1,000 millimeters = 2.54 centimeters
12 inches = 1 foot = 0.3048 meter
3 feet = 1 yard = 0.9144 meter

Square Measure
1 square inch = 6.452 square centimeters
144 square inches = 1 square foot = 929.03 square centimeters
9 square feet = 1 square yard = 0.8361 square meter

Sewing Procedures

Sewing With Felt

Most of the projects detailed call for felt and are illustrated with outside seams. Since felt does not require hemming, constructing a felt project simply requires placing two matching shapes together, right sides facing out, and sewing ⅛ to ¼ inch in from all edges. For stuffed items, leave a bit of the seam unsewn and stuff. Never stuff very firmly if an item has not been assembled with inside seams (see below). If you are using a sewing machine, continue to sew the open seam closed after stuffing rather than using a hand stitch, since felt items tend to be rather flat.

Sewing With Fabric

Almost all of the toys can be made of fabric instead of felt. The difference is that fabric toys have inside seams.

When constructing fabric projects, place two matching shapes together, right sides facing each other. Sew along all edges, ¼ inch in, leaving a small section of seam unsewn. Snip into the seam, up to, but not into, the stitches, around all sharp corners and curves. Turn the item inside out and stuff firmly. Hand sew the open seam closed.

Sewing On Appliqués

Since most appliqués will be made of felt, sew them in place ⅛ inch in from the edges. Fabric appliqués can also be used, but you will have to turn under all raw edges when sewing in place. You can also sew them around their raw edges, using a tight buttonhole stitch if your machine has one.

Gluing On Appliqués

Many smaller appliqués are either too tiny to sew in place or too time consuming if you have to work with a large quantity of them. In both cases, your best bet is to glue them in place using a white glue in an applicator-tip bottle. Squeeze a line of glue on the appliqués, ¼ inch in from all edges. Position appliqués, press flat, and allow them to dry.

Creating Faces

Faces for many of the dolls can be created in a variety of ways. You can glue on felt facial features, or use a combination of felt and embroidered designs. Small buttons can be eyes and yarn can be sewn on for hair. (If you use buttons, secure them as tightly as possible so that young hands cannot pull them off.) Felt-tip markers can also create marvelous faces.

Mixing And Matching

For a little variety, you can mix and match toys from all of the projects: the Watermelon-Seed People might take a plunge into the Bowl of Fruit Punch. You can simply make the toys and eliminate the bags, boards, and pouches they fit into.

1

FAMILIAR DWELLINGS

It takes a floor, a ceiling, and walls to create a dwelling, no matter what it is made of. Equally important is that the space, which holds everything together, is permeated with love and caring, especially when children are part of the family structure. Children have a keen concept of what a house is all about, and here are nine unusual dwellings, with zany tenants, they can experience and love.

Five Little Vegetables Flavor the Soup

Meet the family of vegetables that live in a can of soup.

Try to think of a can of vegetable soup as an inhabited miniature house in the round. You may have to stretch your imagination a bit, but for young children, who turn mud into pies and sand into castles all the time, it's a piece of cake. A child's creativity is boundless, and anything is indeed possible. Let's see, the potato could be the father and the tomato could be the mother. The peas are small enough to be the children, and what about the carrot and the celery stalk? Why not leave these arduous decisions to your little ones.

Soup Can

1. The soup can is constructed of **two 12½-by-20-inch red felt rectangles**. The label is a **10-inch square of white felt**, and the top and bottom borders are each **1-by-12½-inch light blue or gray felt rectangles (cut four)**.

2. The letters and the bowl of soup motif are placed on a grid (1 square = 1 inch). Enlarge the grid and the designs on paper to establish your patterns. Cut out the patterns.

3. Use the patterns to cut one of each design and letter (three of letter E) from **colors of felt**.

4. Arrange the letters on the label and glue or sew them in place.

5. Sew the constructed label to one can shape, about 3½ inches down from a 12½-inch side.

6. Sew a border to the top and bottom of each can shape.

7. Arrange bowl of soup shapes below the label and glue or sew them in place.

8. To construct the can, sew the top edge of each can shape to a **12-inch zipper**. Sew the shapes together along the sides and bottom.

Vegetable Family

1. The vegetables are placed on a grid (1 square = 1 inch). Make the patterns as above.

2. Use the patterns to cut two of each vegetable shape and top greenery from **appropriate felt colors**. Cut out round eyes and the grins from scrap felt.

3. Glue the facial features to one shape of each vegetable. Sew or glue the peas to one pod shape after you have added the faces.

4. Construct the vegetables' top greenery by sewing two of each greenery shape together. You can stuff the greenery slightly for extra body. Sew the star-shaped greenery to the tomato.

5. To create the vegetables, sew each pair of matching shapes together, with its corresponding greenery tucked into the seam. Add a little **stuffing** between the shapes for body.

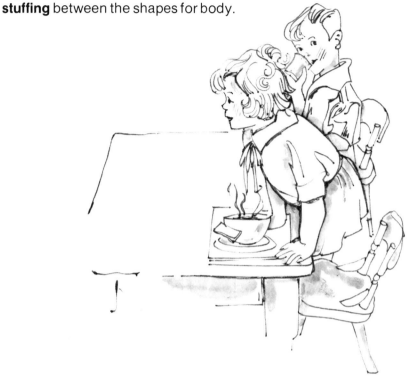

1 square = 1 inch

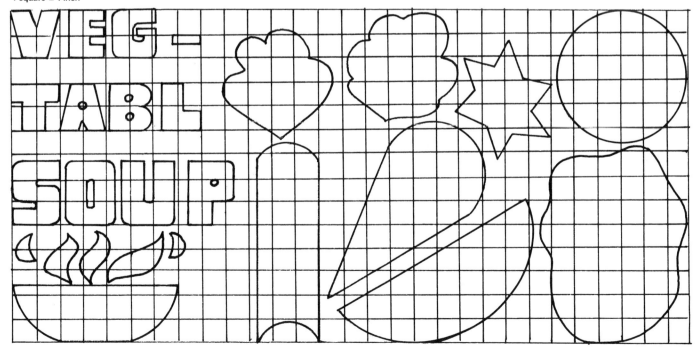

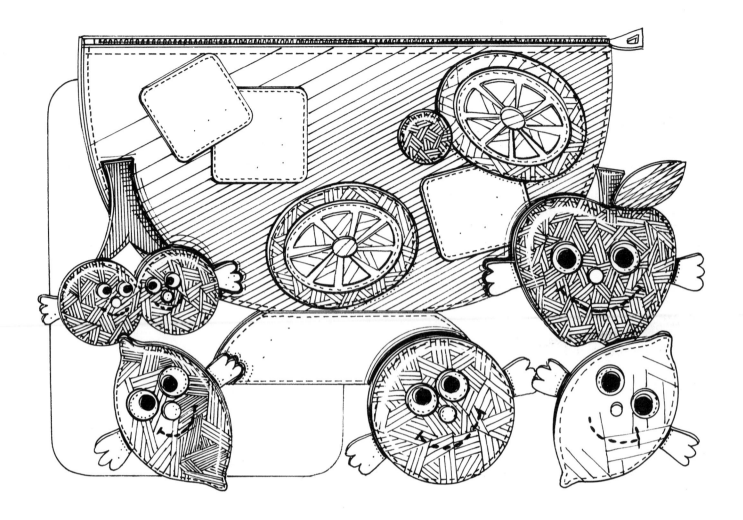

Life is Just a Bowl of Punchy Fruits

It takes more than one fruit to make a great bowl of punch.

Conduct a survey of your children's favorite soft drinks, and fruit punch will rank high on the list. Somehow, when many fruits are blended together, the result is a juice beverage that satisfies the taste buds and satiates the thirst. Since young ones love punch so dearly, your special tots will surely appreciate this bowl filled with their favorite fruits.

P.S. Remember to add the ice cubes.

Fruit

1. The fruits are placed on a grid (1 square = ½ inch). Enlarge the grid and the designs on paper to establish your patterns. Cut out the patterns.

2. Use the patterns to cut out the fruits in their **appropriate felt colors**. Cut out the hands freehand. The hands can be any color or simply all white.

3. Cut out white and black circle eyes and a white circle nose for each fruit.

4. Sew or glue the eyes and nose on one shape of fruit. Mouths can be cut from felt or embroidered on.

5. Sew the matching fruit shapes together, with a bit of **stuffing** between them. Tuck the hands into the seams before you sew. Add a stem and a green leaf (cut freehand) to the apple.

Punch Bowl

1. Study the diagram, then draw the punch bowl and its base on a 7-by-12½-inch paper rectangle. It is a large semi-oval resting on a smaller semi-oval. Cut out the pattern.

2. Using the pattern, cut two bowl shapes from **pink or red felt**.

3. Cut two additional base shapes from **white felt**, using the base portion of the bowl pattern as your guide.

4. Sew a base shape over the base portion of each punch bowl shape.

5. The ice cubes, cherries, and orange slices can be cut freehand from **appropriate felt colors**. Or, use the exact patterns, which are placed on a grid (1 square = ½ inch). Enlarge the grid and the designs on paper to establish your patterns. Cut out the patterns and use them to cut the fruit and ice cube appliqués from colored felt.

6. Sew the ice cubes, cherries, and orange slices on both punch bowl shapes.

7. Sew the top straight sides of the bowl shapes to a **12-inch zipper**.

8. Sew the bowl shapes together along the remaining sides.

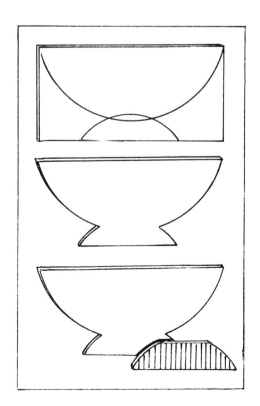

1 square = ½ inch

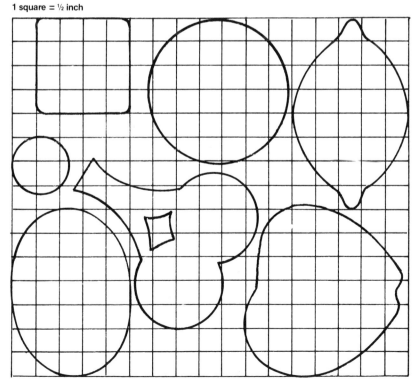

The Seed People Live in a Slice of Watermelon

Tuck watermelon seeds where they belong, inside a slice of watermelon.

Children love to eat ripe, juicy watermelon, but oh! those annoying seeds. With every bite comes a mouthful of slippery black pits that somehow inhabit every nook and cranny of your home until long after the melon season has ended. Here is a slice of watermelon that looks delicious enough to eat but contains the friendliest bunch of seeds your favorite youngsters will ever encounter.

Watermelon-Seed Dolls

1. Trace one watermelon-seed doll directly from the book onto tracing paper to establish your pattern. Cut out the pattern.

2. Use the pattern to cut out two doll shapes from black felt.

3. Sew round eyes topped with **black buttons or black felt circles** on

one doll shape. Also sew on a **pink felt mouth.**

4. Sew the two doll shapes together, facial features facing out. Leave a small section of the seam at the top unsewn for stuffing.

5. **Stuff**, then hand stitch the open seam closed.

6. Repeat three or four times for more seed dolls.

Watermelon Slice

1. Evenly round two corners of the long side of an 11-by-18½-inch paper rectangle, and use this as the watermelon-slice pattern.

2. Cut two melon shapes from **green felt** using the pattern.

3. Now cut away 2½ inches from the paper pattern along the sides and rounded bottom (do not cut paper away from the top straight edge).

4. Use the trimmed pattern to cut one shape from **white felt**.

5. Trim away an additional 1 inch from the sides and rounded bottom of the paper pattern, as above.

6. Use this pattern to cut one shape from **red felt**. (You now have three pieces—green, white, and red—cut in the same shape but successively smaller.)

7. Cut a few seeds freehand from **black felt**.

8. Center the white shape on a green shape, top edges flush, and sew them together.

9. Scatter the black seeds on the red shape and glue or sew them in place.

10. Center the red shape on the white shape, top edges flush, and sew them together.

11. Sew the top straight edge of the assembled slice and the remaining slice to an **18-inch zipper**.

12. Sew the two slice shapes together along the sides and rounded bottom.

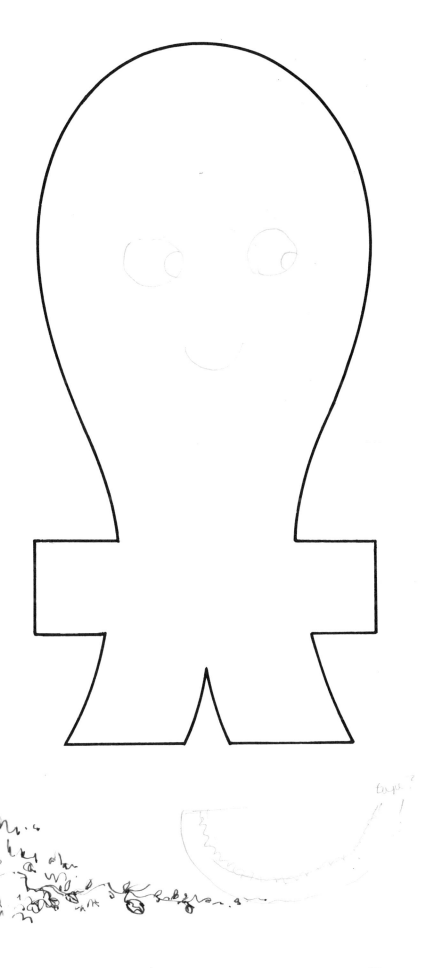

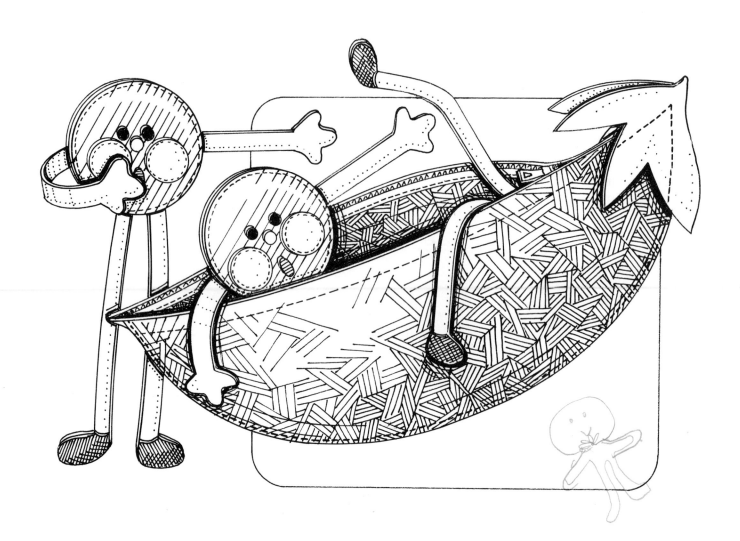

Three Silly Friends That Call A Pea Pod Home

There's nothing cozier than three peas in a pod.

There's an old expression that best typifies a snug situation: "Like three peas in a pod." If you have ever been one of three passengers in the front seat of a car or on an amusement park ride, then you know what closeness is all about. The three peas in this pod do not mind the cozy surroundings because they won't be spending much time in it, especially once little hands discover them.

Peas

1. Cut two 3½-inch circles from green felt.

2. Cut two simple 3½-inch-long arms with hands and 6-inch-long legs with feet.

3. From **felt** cut two **pink** cheeks, a

white nose, and two **black** eyes. Cut two black shoes for each leg.

4. Sew or glue the facial features to one circle and two shoes sandwiching each foot.

5. Tuck the arms and legs into the circles. Sew the circles together with a bit of **stuffing** between them.

6. Repeat for the other two peas and zip all three into their pod.

Pea Pod

1. The pea pod and its leaf cap are placed on a grid (1 square = 1 inch). Enlarge the grid and the designs on paper to establish your patterns. Cut out the patterns.

2. Use the patterns to cut two pea-pod shapes from **green felt** and two leaf caps from a **lighter green felt**.

3. Sew the inside curve of the pod shapes to respective sides of a **24-inch zipper**.

4. Sew the pod shapes together along the outer curved sides.

5. Place the leaf cap shapes together, with one end of the pod between them. Sew in place.

1 square = 1 inch

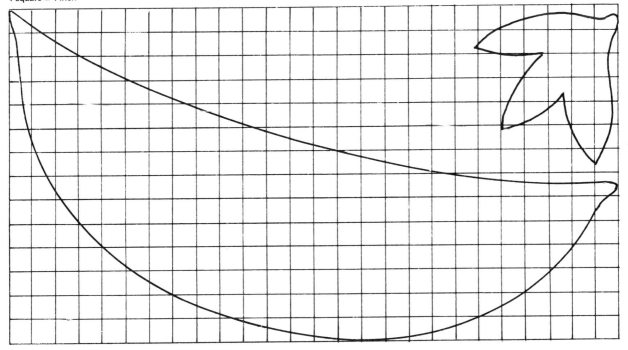

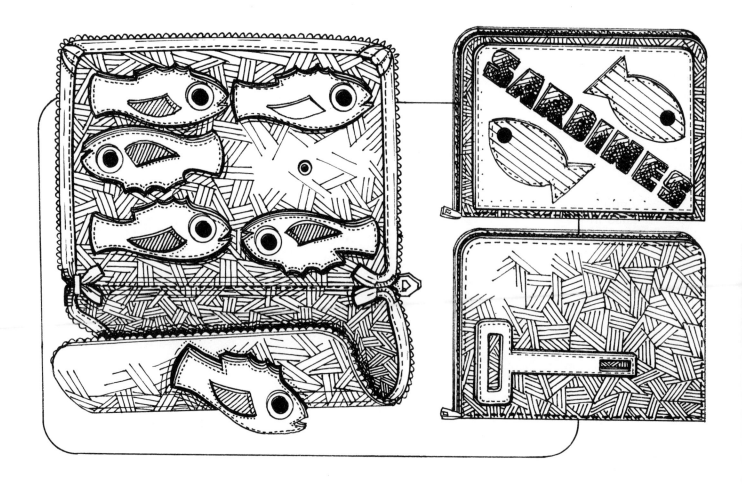

A Can of Sardines Children Will Love

A sardine's life is a close encounter of the first kind.

Pea pods may be cozy, but whenever people find themselves in *crowded* places, they invariably compare the environment to a can of sardines. Sardines, actually small herrings, spend their living days swimming in tightly woven schools only to rest in peace, side by side, in tightly packed, oily cans. Children do not have a natural love of sardines, nor do they have a high tolerance for crowded situations; but this special can of fish will have your youngsters coming back for more. Make sure you give these six adorable sardines enough room to be snapped into place.

Sardine Can

1. The sardine can is constructed of two 7-by-10-inch gray rectangles.

Round two corners along one side of each rectangle.

2. Sew the bottoms of **six sewing snaps**, equally spaced in two rows of three, to one can shape.

3. Cut a third rectangle, slightly smaller than the can shapes, from **white felt**; this will be the label. Round two corners on one length.

4. The label's designs and the key are their actual sizes in the drawing. Trace them directly from the book onto tracing paper to establish your patterns. Cut out the patterns.

5. Use the patterns to cut the key, letters, and fish from **colors of felt**.

6. Construct the label by gluing or sewing the word SARDINE and the fish on the white rectangle.

7. Sew the label to the back side of

the can shape that holds the snap halves. Sew the key to the other can shape.

8. Sew the two can shapes together along their straight side, designs facing out.

9. Open the sewn can shapes flat. Place the bottom of an opened **24-inch zipper** on one end of the stitched seam. Baste each half of the zipper around the entire edge of its respective side. Ease in the zipper around the corners, as they will buckle slightly.

10. Once the zipper has been basted to the sides, permanently sew in place.

Sardines

1. Trace the sardine directly from the book onto tracing paper to establish your pattern. Cut out the pattern.

2. Use the pattern to cut two sardine shapes from **light green or blue felt**. Then cut a fin from the same color felt.

3. Glue a white and **black felt** circle eye to each fish shape. Add the fin to only one shape.

4. Sew the two fish shapes together with a little **stuffing** between them, eyes facing out.

5. Repeat for a total of six sardines.

6. Place the six fish inside the can to determine how to position the corresponding halves of the snaps. Sew the snaps in place on the side of the fish that doesn't have the fin.

7. Snap the fish in place and zip up the can!

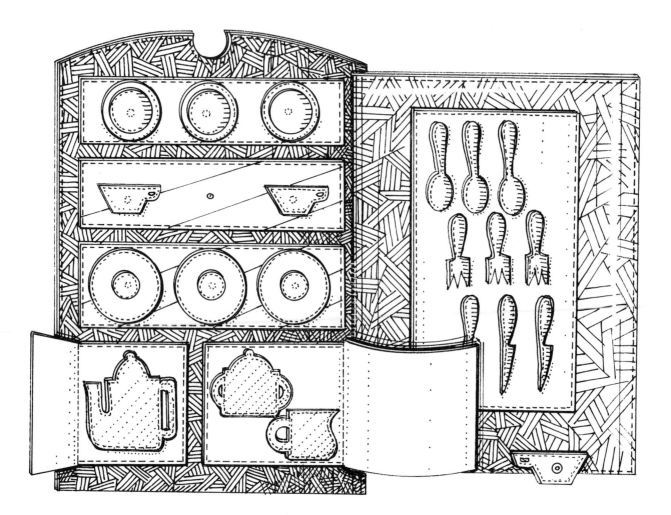

Mother Hubbard's Tea Service Cupboard

Old Mother Hubbard's cupboard was never this neat; nor was her refrigerator ever so full.

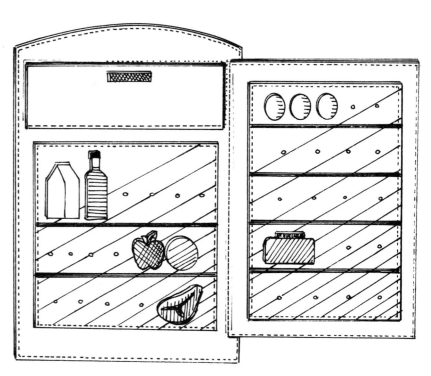

As the nursery rhyme concludes, the cupboard was bare and Old Mother Hubbard's little pooch went hungry. No explanation was offered for the empty shelves and one can only deduce that there must have been one deep recession at the time the rhyme was written. Things are much better today, as your little ones will see when they open their own cupboard and refrigerator. Everything is neatly snapped in place, and now may be a good time to teach your tots ". . . a place for everything and everything in its place."

Tea Service Cupboard

1. Construct the cupboard of two 13-by-19-inch **brown felt** rectangles. One width of each shape should be curved and have a small circle cut out of it for decoration.

2. Make the cupboard door of two 12½-by-17-inch **brown felt** rectangles.

3. Cut three shelves from a **light-colored felt**; they should measure 11 inches by 2½, 3, and 3½ inches wide respectively. Also cut the bottom cabinets and their doors, 5 inches high and 5 and 6 inches wide respectively.

4. The door's flatware display panel is a 7-by-12-inch rectangle cut from a **light colored felt**.

5. Pin the shelves and cabinets to one cupboard shape. Pin the display panel to one door shape.

6. Sew the shelves, cabinets, and the display panel in place.

7. Sew the doors over their corresponding cabinets.

8. Sew the bottom halves of **large sewing snaps** to the shelves, cabinets, and display panel. Use enough to accommodate all of the pieces of the tea service and the flatware you intend to make.

9. Sew the two cupboard shapes together. For extra body, add a thin layer of **batting or interfacing** between the shapes before sewing.

10. Sew the two door shapes together. Add quilt batting or interfacing if you wish extra body.

11. Sew the door to the cupboard along the left side.

Tea Service

1. The pieces of the tea service and the flatware are placed on a grid (1 square = 1 inch). Enlarge the grid and the designs on paper to establish your patterns. Cut out the patterns.

2. Use the patterns to cut out the individual tea service and flatware pieces from **assorted colors of felt**. Cut out two shapes for each piece.

3. Sew each matching pair of shapes together. You can add batting or interfacing between the shapes for extra body.

4. Sew the remaining halves of the snaps to the backs of the constructed pieces.

5. Snap the tea service and the flatware in place and close the doors.

Refrigerator

The refrigerator is cut and constructed following the same instructions as the cupboard, except that it is cut from **white felt**, the cut circle is eliminated from the curved side, and there are three different-size **gray felt** food compartments. The smallest rectangle is the freezer compartment, and you will need a white felt door to fit over it.

Sew the food compartments to their respective white-felt shapes. Sew the freezer door over the freezer compartment along one side. Create shelves by sewing lengths of narrow, dark-colored **ribbon** across the widths of the rectangles. Design your own food items and cut them from **assorted colors of felt**. Sew snap halves to refrigerator and foods, and snap them in place as you did the tea service.

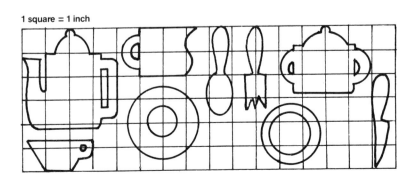

1 square = 1 inch

A Dollar Bill, or Its Many Different Coins

Learning the value of a dollar makes good sense.

Young ones are constantly asking for change to satisfy their insatiable needs. Juvenile bankers know how to spend a dollar, but what happened to the old addage, "A penny saved is a penny earned"? Now is a good time to teach your youngsters the value of money with this learning dollar, which doubles as a zip-open pouch for all the coins.

Dollar

1. Construct the dollar from two 7-by-12½-inch **green felt** rectangles. From **white felt**, cut a center rectangle of 4 by 8 inches.

2. Place appliqué designs for the dollar on a grid (1 square = ¾ inch). Enlarge the grid and the designs on paper to establish your patterns, then cut out the patterns.

3. Use the patterns to cut the ap-

pliqués from light shades of **green and gray felt**.

4. Machine-stitch the white rectangle to one dollar shape, ¾ inch away from one long side, and centered width-wise. Sew or glue the appropriate appliqués to the white rectangle.

5. Arrange the remaining appliqués on the dollar shape and glue or sew them in place.

6. Sew the top of the two dollar shapes to a **12-inch zipper**.

7. Sew the remaining three sides of the dollar together.

Coins

1. Cut silver coins from **gray or light blue felt**. Copper pennies are cut from **light brown felt**. The 50-cent coin is a 4½-inch circle, the 25-cent coin is 3½ inches, the 5-cent coin is 3 inches, and the pennies are 2½ inches. Use a compass to help you draw circles.

2. Cut two circles for each coin.

3. The numbers for the coins are placed on a grid (1 square = ¾ inch). Make patterns as above. Cut out the numbers from white felt.

4. Sew each pair of circles together with a bit of **stuffing** between them. Glue on the corresponding numbers.

5. Make any assortment of coins that will add up to one dollar.

1 square = ¾ inch

A-Penny-a-Wish Well

At the bottom of this well lies a handful of pennies.

The all-important backyard well of days gone by had the distinction of being the depository of wishes and dreams come true. As custom has it, a coin was sacrificed to the well in return for a favor. No one actually knows when this romantic ritual began, but it has been a point of interest for novelists and playwrights alike. The wishing well has crept into children's literature as well, and what youngster wouldn't love to have one of his or her very own. Here's a personalized small version of this symbol of fantasy. The new tradition is that every wish costs a penny. If the wishes never materialize, there will always be a handful of pennies at the bottom of the well.

Well

1. The wishing well is constructed of two sections; the roof and the well itself. Cut two 3½-by-8-inch **red felt** rectangles for the roof. Cut the short sides at an angle. Then cut two 6½-inch squares from **light blue felt** for the well.

2. For the stone walls, cut two **light blue or gray felt** 2-by-6½-inch rectangles.

3. Cut irregular-shaped stones from a **dark color felt**. Sew or glue them to one side of each wall shape.

4. Sew the longer side of a roof shape, centered, to each well shape.

5. Sew a stone wall shape to the bottom of each well shape.

6. Cut a pole from **brown felt** and a bucket from **black felt**, freehand, for each side of the well. Also cut out a brown handle.

7. Glue or sew a pole and bucket to each well shape.

8. Cut out the area between the handle and the top of the bucket, through both layers of felt; this will be the coin slot.

9. Sew the bottom of each well shape to one side of a **6-inch zipper**.

10. Sew the remaining sides of the well together. Slip the handle into the seam, in line with the pole, as you sew.

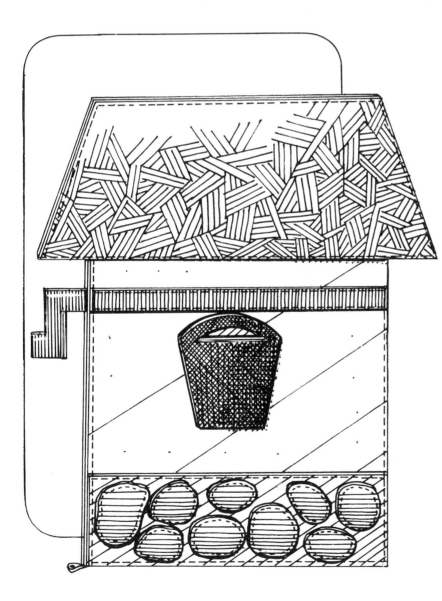

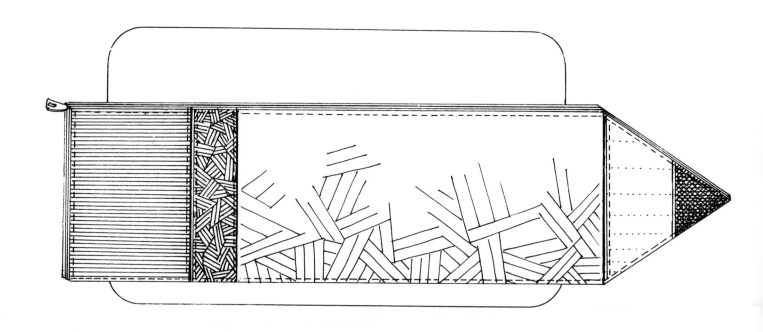

A Pencil Case is a Sharp Idea

Pencils will never be lost if they are always kept safely in a pencil case.

Pencils and peanuts have one thing in common—you can never have enough of them. Children seem to devour pencils on their daily journey to and from school, and this phenomenon can become pretty frustrating and expensive. And when was the last time you saw a seven-inch pencil whittle down to a one-inch stub? Here's a solution that's worth a try: encourage your children to always put their pencils inside their zippered pencil case after the homework and drawing activities have ended.

Pencil Case

1. Cut two 2-by-8-inch rectangles from **yellow felt** for the body of the pencil. Cut one end of each rectangle into a point so that the rectangles match.

2. Cut two 1½-by-2-inch rectangles from **pink felt** for the eraser, and two 3¾-by-2-inch rectangles from **gray felt** for the metal band.

3. The pencil's point is constructed of two triangles—**a light brown** for the wood, topped by a small **black** triangle for the graphite tip. They should

be cut to fit on the point of the pencil.

4. Sew the triangles to the point of each pencil shape.

5. Sew the pink rectangles and the gray rectangles to the end opposite the point of each pencil shape.

6. Sew one length of each pencil shape to a **6-inch zipper**.

7. Sew the remaining sides of the pencil together.

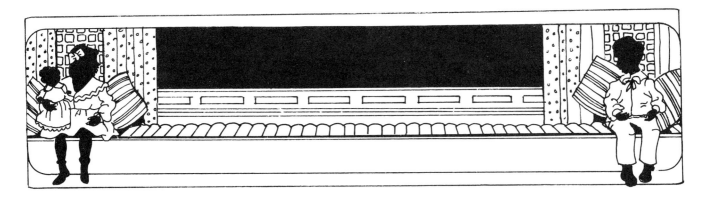

2

POPULAR FRIENDS

If it is true that children will eat a pound of dirt before they grow up to be adults, it is equally true that they will cultivate a bushel of friends during this growing period. Friends come and go as new situations develop: attending a new school, moving to a new neighborhood, or going away for the summer. Some of the most pleasant childhood friendships are the imaginary ones. Just think of having a salt shaker, a tooth fairy, a swinging bear, or a fairy godmother for a best friend. Children can.

Fun is a Barrel Filled With Monkeys

It takes more than just one monkey to fill up this barrel.

What could be more fun than a barrel of monkeys? Watching little children playing with them. This fabric cask contains a bunch of primates that have curved arms and legs for swinging upside down, right-side up, alone, or in a hooked chain. When all of the fun and silliness is finished for the day, the monkeys are neatly zipped into their adorable barrel.

Bunch of Monkeys

1. The monkey is placed on a grid (1 square = ¾ inch). Enlarge the grid and the design on paper to establish your pattern. Cut out the pattern.

2. Use the pattern to cut two monkey shapes from **brown felt or fabric**.

3. Cut inner ears, facial features, and a tummy from **colors of felt**. Glue or sew them in place on one monkey shape.

4. Place the two monkey shapes together, right sides facing, and sew along all sides, leaving 1 inch of seam unsewn at the leg. Turn inside out.

5. Stuff the monkey firmly and hand-stitch the open seam closed.

6. Make many monkeys.

Barrel

1. Cut two 13-by-18-inch rectangles from **brown felt or fabric**. Curve both lengths to form a barrel shape. The width of the barrel should measure 8½ inches long.

2. Cut strips from **gray felt** for the top and bottom bands. You can have an additional band across the middle.

3. Sew the bands to both barrel shapes.

4. Sew one side of each barrel shape to an **8-inch zipper**. Continue to sew the barrel shapes together along the remaining sides.

1 square = ¾ inch

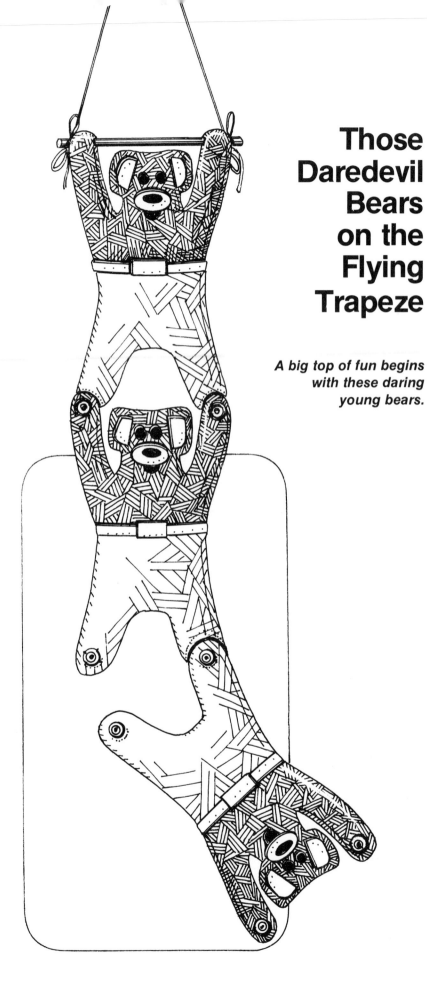

Those Daredevil Bears on the Flying Trapeze

A big top of fun begins with these daring young bears.

One of the main attractions at a large circus is the bear act. How they can train those big bruins to perform tricks is quite incomprehensible. These bears do not cha cha or tango, but they are daredevils of the flying trapeze. With snaps sewn to their hands and feet, they can be attached in every which way to execute a myriad of tricks.

Bears

1. The bear pattern is given the actual size in the drawing. Trace the designs on paper to establish your patterns. Cut out the patterns.

2. Use the patterns to cut two tops from **brown fabric or felt** and two bottoms from **pink felt**.

3. To construct a bear shape, sew a top to a bottom. Make two shapes.

4. For a fabric bear, place two body shapes together, right sides facing, and sew along all edges, leaving a section of the seam unsewn at the waist. Turn inside out. For a felt bear, sew together, right sides facing out.

5. **Stuff** the bear firmly and hand-stitch the open seam closed.

6. Cut a belt, buckle, inner ears, eyes, snout, and mouth from **appropriate colors of felt scraps**. Glue in place.

7. Make many bears.

8. Cut a few stitches in the seams of both hands of one bear, near the top.

9. Push a length of ¼-**inch wooden dowel** into the open seams of both hands.

10. Tie **a length of cord** to both ends of the dowel for hanging.

11. Sew one half of a **sewing snap** to each foot of the bear with the dowel.

12. Sew the matching halves to the hands of another bear, at the back.

13. Sew snap halves to both the front and back of the hands and feet of the remaining bears.

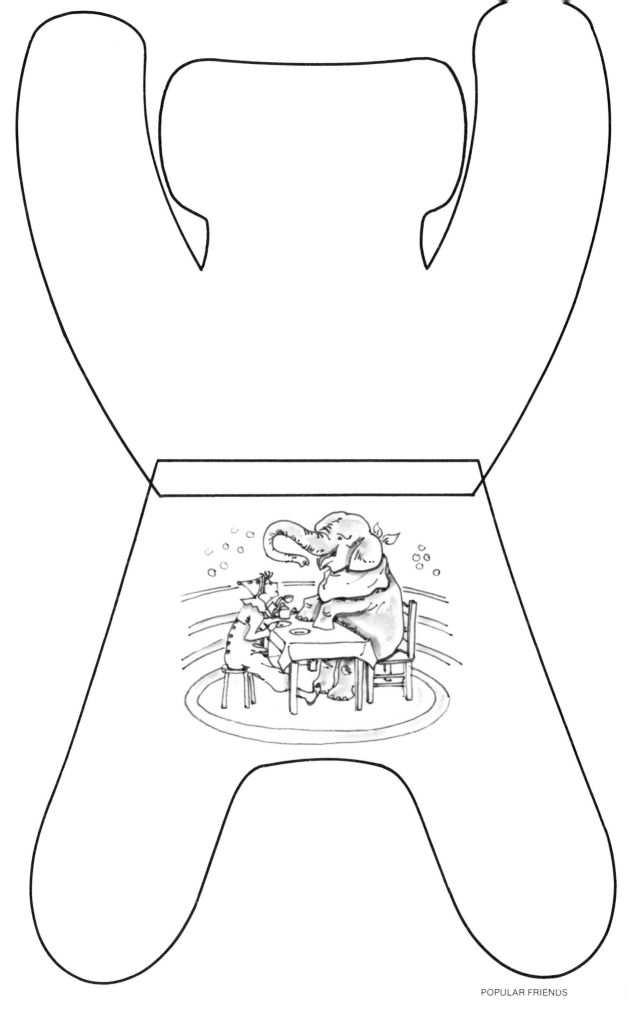

A Perky Pair of Pouch Partners

Did you know that sea horses and kangaroos are born in pouches?

Sea horses and kangaroos have surprisingly one thing in common: they both begin life in a pouch. Most people know all about the kangaroo, but do you know that the female sea horse deposits her eggs into her partner's pouch, where they are fertilized and remain until they hatch? Children will find this similarity of nature very strange at first, but it will be a fact they will never forget as they play with these cute pouched dolls.

Sea Horses

1. The sea horses are placed on a grid (1 square = ¾ inch). Enlarge the grid and the designs on paper to establish your patterns. Cut out the patterns.

2. Use the patterns to cut two shapes of each sea horse from **a solid or a print fabric**. The fins and pocket are cut from a **compatible color felt**.

3. Place each matching pair of sea horse shapes together, right sides facing. Tuck the fins into the seams, on the back, and sew along all edges, leaving a section of seam unsewn below the fins.

4. Turn both sea horses inside out, **stuff** firmly, and hand-stitch the open seams closed.

5. Hand-stitch the pouch to the larger sea horse, along the sides and bottom.

6. Glue or sew on eyes to both sea horses.

7. Slip the baby into the pouch.

Kangaroos

1. Enlarge the grid and patterns for both kangaroos. Cut out the patterns and use them to cut two of each kangaroo shape from **light brown felt**. Cut out four arms and legs for each.

2. Construct the body of each kangaroo just as you did the sea horses. Add the pouch to the larger kangaroo.

3. Sew every two matching legs and arms together, right sides facing, leaving a small section of seam unsewn on each.

4. Turn each arm and leg inside out, stuff firmly, and hand-stitch the open seams closed.

5. Hand-stitch the arms and legs to the larger kangaroo.

6. The arms and legs of the smaller kangaroo are single-ply appliqués sewn in place.

7. Cut out two eyes and ears from **appropriate colors of felt**. Sew or glue in place.

8. Slip the baby inside the pouch.

1 square = ¾ inch

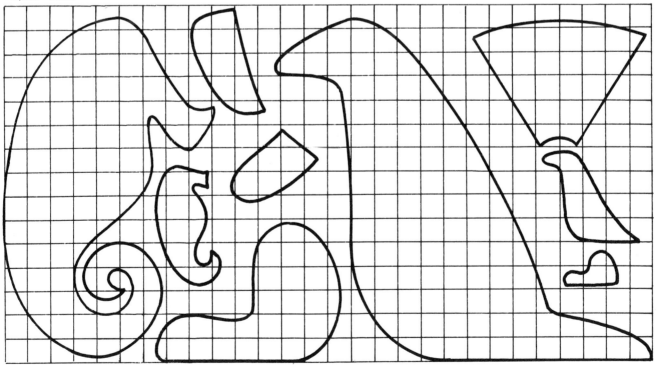

Salt and Pepper Shakers With Personalities

Foods would taste mighty bland if it were not for salt and pepper.

Salt and pepper are a popular duo that are found wherever foods are prepared and served. There probably isn't a household in the world where you would not find a shaker or two of these essential flavorings. Both have unique qualities and personalities of their own. Salt is, well, rather salty, and pepper is the hot stuff. By now your little ones are quite familiar with this tasty twosome, and here's a salt-and-pepper-shaker set they can enjoy for hours of fun.

Shakers

1. The body for the salt and pepper shakers has a 5-inch base, a height of 5½ inches, and a 3-inch-wide top (see drawing). Draw the body shape on paper to establish your pattern. Cut out the pattern.

2. Use the body pattern to cut four **white** and four **black felt** shapes.

3. The arms and legs are 2-by-3-inch rectangles with one width rounded. The head is a 4-by-5-inch rectangle with one rounded width. Draw both shapes on paper to establish your patterns. Cut out the patterns.

4. Cut eight arm and eight leg shapes and two head shapes from **white felt** for each doll.

5. The shakers' designs are shown same-size in the drawing. Trace them on tracing paper to establish your patterns. Cut out the patterns.

6. Use the patterns to cut the vertical details from **gray felt**, and the labels and letters from any other **color of felt**. The chili-pepper heart is **red** and the pretzel heart is **brown**.

7. Sew every two arm and two leg shapes together and each pair of head shapes together, with a bit of **stuffing** between them.

8. Sew or glue the pretzel heart to one white body shape.

9. Place the body shape with the pretzel on another white shape, and sew together along the top, right side and bottom, tucking the head, one arm and two legs into their proper places.

10. Lightly stuff the body through the open side. Tuck the remaining arm into the side in its proper position.

11. Sew the shaker's vertical appliqués to another white body shape. Sew the label, with the word SALT glued or sewn in place, over the vertical appliqués.

12. Sew the appliquéd shape to the remaining white shape along the top, side, and bottom.

13. Place the shape with the label on top of the stuffed shape with the heart. Line up all edges.

14. Sew both constructed shapes together along the left side.

15. Glue dark felt circles and gray cap holes to the head.

16. Construct PEPPER just as you did SALT, but with a red-pepper heart.

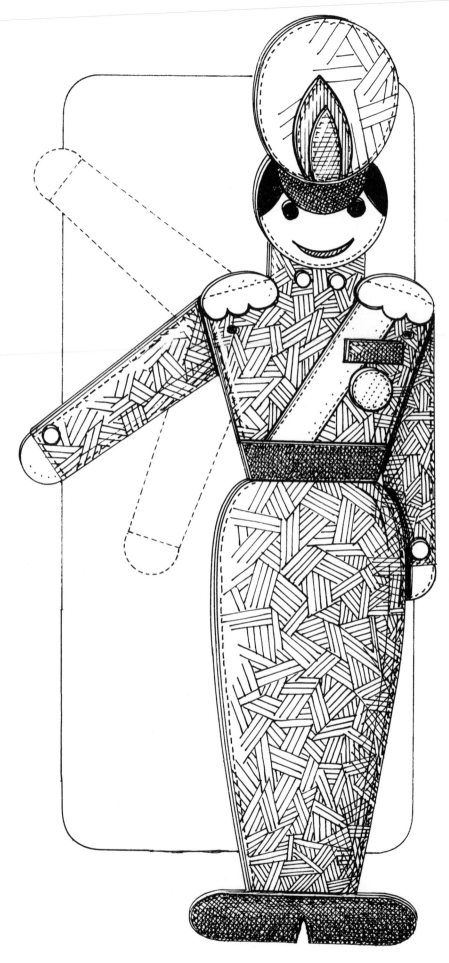

An Army of Soldiers for a Junior Platoon Chief

Clean the barracks and get the troops ready; It's time to present arms.

"You're in the army now," is what you will be singing to the young recipient of this exciting, action toy. It has anywhere from one to a platoon of soldiers ready to take orders and serve their junior commanding officer. The soldiers' arms pivot so they can salute, stand at attention, and present arms. When the field exercises are over for the day, they are zipped into their quarters for the evening.

Toy Soldier

1. The soldier is shown full-size in the drawing. Trace the body, head, hat, shoe, and arm shapes on tracing paper to establish your patterns. Note that the neck is drawn straight (under the head), the head is a full circle (under the hat), and the top of the arms are squared (behind the shoulders). Cut out the patterns.

2. Use the patterns to cut out **two blue felt** bodies, **four blue** arms, **two skin-tone** heads, **two black** shoes, and **two yellow** hats. You will also need two hands, two belts, two shoulder epaulets, and four buttons

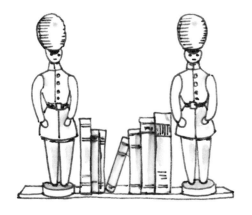

in **appropriate colors of felt**. All other details require one of each (see drawing).

3. Sew or glue the appropriate appliqués to each body shape. The shoes and belts are sewn to both shapes.

4. Place the body shapes together, right sides facing out, and sew along all edges, leaving a section of seam unsewn on one leg.

5. **Stuff** the soldier and hand-stitch the open seam closed.

6. Glue or embroider the facial features to one head shape.

7. Place the two head shapes together with the neck of the body shapes sandwiched between them. Sew together with a bit of **stuffing** between the head shapes.

8. Glue or sew the feather and the visor to one hat shape.

9. Place the two hat shapes together, with the top of the head sandwiched between them. Sew together with a bit of stuffing between the hat shapes.

10. Place each pair of arm shapes together with a hand tucked into the bottom seam. Sew around the edges with a bit of **stuffing** between them.

11. Sew the bottom of a **large sewing snap** at the center of the top of each arm.

12. Sew matching snap halves to the back of the soldier, at the shoulders.

13. Snap both arms in place.

14. Make an army of soldiers.

Soldier's Guardhouse

1. The size of the guardhouse depends on how many soldiers you make. Cut two rectangles, with one end cut into a point, from **white felt**. Try to make the bottom edge large enough to accommodate a **standard-size zipper**.

2. Sew strips of **red felt or fabric ribbon** on the diagonal, across one rectangle.

3. Sew a felt door with a rounded top to the center of the rectangle with the stripes.

4. Sew the bottom edge of each rectangle to a zipper.

5. Continue to sew the guardhouse together along the remaining sides.

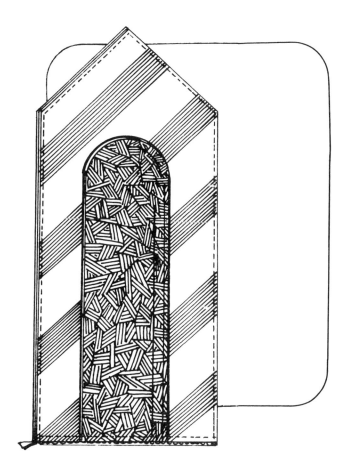

Jack Frost is the Keeper of the Snowflakes

On a cold winter's day, Jack Frost is a warm and cuddly friend.

It takes a mighty cold day for Jack Frost to come tapping on your window. You know he's there because he adorns the window panes in his crystalized attire. Children are naturally mesmerized by the intricate patterns that seem to be etched into the glass. This Jack Frost doll has a magic pocket that contains one-of-a-kind snowflakes. He will warm and cuddle any youngster when the north wind is howling its chilling lament.

Jack Frost

1. Jack Frost is placed on a grid (1 square = 1 inch). Enlarge the grid and the designs on paper to establish your patterns. Cut out the patterns.

2. Use the patterns to cut two body shapes, eyebrows, mustache, and wind swirls from **white felt**.

3. Cut the face from a **skin-tone felt**,

1 square = 1 inch

and cut out a **pink nose** and a **red mouth**.

4. Sew the face and the wind swirls to one body shape. Glue on the remaining facial features.

5. From **white felt**, cut a pocket that is large enough to fit on a body shape.

6. Sew the pocket to the appliquéd body shape, below the wind swirls.

7. Place the two body shapes together, appliquéd side facing out, and sew along all edges, leaving a section of seam unsewn at the side.

8. Stuff the doll and sew the open seam closed.

Lacy Snowflakes

1. From **felt or paper**, cut a circle that is large enough to fit into Jack's pocket.

2. Fold the circle in half.

3. Fold the halved circle in three equal sections.

4. Fold the folded circle in half again.

5. Cut out shapes from the sides and top edge of the folded circle.

6. Unfold the snowflake to see the design you have created.

7. Make many snowflakes, and arrange them in Jack's pocket.

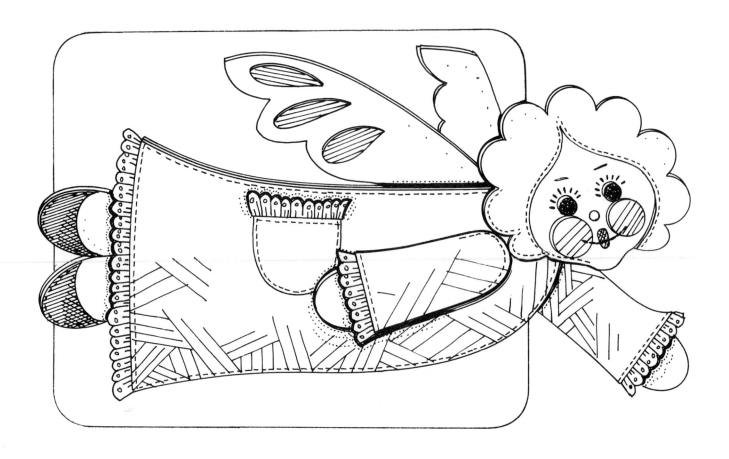

A "Personal Delivery" Tooth Fairy

A tooth in the pocket is worth a quarter under the pillow.

When a child loses a tooth, it is usually not traumatic because of the reward it will bring. Here is a new twist on an old tradition. A tooth is placed in the pocket of this tooth fairy doll, and sleeps alongside your little one. When Mommy or Daddy, that is, the tooth fairy, comes to make the swap, it is easy to find in the dark. In the morning, the pocket is opened and out rolls a shiny new coin.

Tooth Fairy

1. The tooth fairy is placed on a grid (1 square = ½ inch). Enlarge the grid and the designs on paper to establish your patterns. Cut out the patterns.

2. Use the patterns to cut one **white felt** wing, a **skin tone** head, and a **yellow felt** hair shape. Cut out two of each **skin tone** hands and feet, **white** body shapes, and two **black** shoes.

3. Sew the crown of hair to her head. Glue or sew on felt facial features.

4. Sew a hand to each arm, topped with **narrow pregathered lace**.

5. Sew a shoe to each foot.

6. Sew pregathered lace to the base edge of one body shape.

7. Cut a pocket from **white felt** and sew pregathered lace to the top edge.

8. Sew the pocket to the body shape with the lace edge. Sew an arm to the shoulder.

9. Place the two body shapes together, right sides facing out, and sew along all edges, tucking the wings, feet, and remaining arm into the seams. Leave an inch of the seam of the skirt unsewn.

10. **Stuff** the doll and sew the open seam closed.

11. Sew the head to the body.

12. Glue on wing details, cut freehand, if you wish.

1 square = ½ inch

Dear
    Fairy
        Godmother,
I wish mom
would make me
some Chocolate
chip cookies.
        Love,
            George

Meet Your Fairy Godmother

With a wave of her wand, life's little problems magically disappear and wishes come true.

As legend has it, when the road to happiness is under construction or when something desired is out of reach, your fairy godmother is ready and willing to lend a helping hand. Wouldn't it be wonderful if life were so simple? Now is a good time to introduce your youngsters to their fairy godmother. Have your youngsters write wishes on paper and zip them into this MAGICAL DOLL. When

she waves her magic wand, frowns turn to smiles and wishes come true.

Fairy Godmother

1. The fairy godmother is placed on a grid (1 square = ½ inch). Enlarge the grid and the designs on paper to establish your patterns. Cut out the patterns.

2. Use the patterns to cut two body

shapes from a **light color of felt**, and two wing shapes from **white felt**. Cut four arms and two 3-inch circles from a **skin-tone felt**.

3. Sew each pair of arms together, with a bit of **stuffing** between them.

4. Sew or glue facial features to one circle. Sew the two circles together with a bit of stuffing between them.

5. Sew the wings to one body shape and glue a heart to the other.

6. Sew the bottom edge of each body shape to a **6-inch zipper**.

7. Sew the body shapes together along the remaining sides, tucking the arms and head into the seams.

8. Gather a **scalloped-edge, eyelet fabric** into a skirt. Sew the skirt around the waist.

9. Sew narrow, **pregathered lace** around the head.

10. For a wand, squiggle a snowflake design on a **net fabric**, using **white glue in an applicator-tip bottle**. Sprinkle **glitter** on it. When dry, cut it out and glue it to a **thin wooden dowel**.

11. Push the dowel into the seam of one hand.

1 square = ½ inch

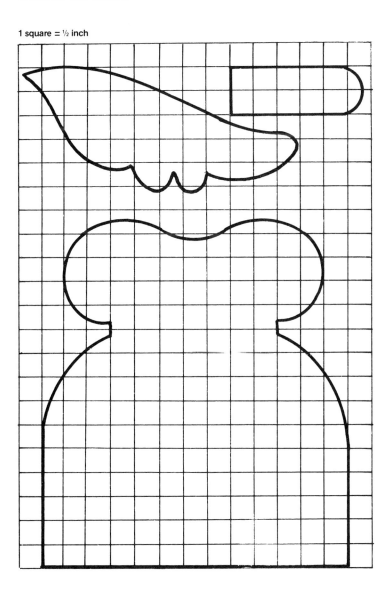

1 square = ½ inch

Mister Sandman is a Pillow Friend

There will be no more sleepless nights as long as Mister Sandman is around.

Mister Sandman will be sending your restless tots off to Dreamland when it's time for them to go to sleep. It is not certain how his magic powers work, but in the case of this doll, just being close by must be the secret. He slips into a pocket that is sewn on a pillowcase, and keeps a watchful eye on his owner.

Mister Sandman

1. Hem the raw edges of a 4-by-5-inch fabric rectangle, and sew it to a pillowcase near the open end. This is the pocket.

2. Mister Sandman and his robe are placed on a grid (1 square = ½ inch). Enlarge the grid and the designs on paper to establish your patterns. Cut out the patterns.

3. Use the patterns to cut two body

shapes from a **skin tone washable fabric**, and two robe and two hat shapes from **blue felt**.

4. Place the two body shapes together, right sides facing, and sew along all edges, leaving a section of seam unsewn on one leg.

5. Turn the doll inside out and **stuff** firmly. Hand-stitch the open seam closed.

6. Draw a face and hair on the head with **indelible felt-tip markers**, or embroider on a face.

7. Sew the two robe shapes together along the sides. Sew the two hat shapes together.

8. Cut a short slit down the robe's neck opening at the back.

9. Sew **bias tape** around all raw edges of the hat and robe.

10. Glue **white felt** stars and a **yellow felt** half moon to the front of the robe, and a star to the hat. Dress the doll.

3

TRAVEL FUN

Children stand waiting to discover what life is all about, as new adventures loom beyond the horizon in every direction. Imagination is the ticket to the world: it will take them soaring above the clouds, sailing on the high seas, steaming through the backwoods on a speeding train, and learning about the experiences of daily living in their own backyard.

A Pirate Ship for Little Buccaneers, and a Sailboat to Chase

Weigh the anchor, there's a treasure chest aboard this pirate ship.

Looking for buried treasure is a common fantasy game among children, due mainly to the scores of movies and volumes of literature devoted to the renegades of the high seas, the pirates. If you have ever observed children at a beach, you will have noticed them burying bogus trinkets in the sand for a lost coin or two. Hoist the anchor and set your little ones on an adventure to a deserted island with this pirate ship. Inside it is a trunk, which contains a treasure chest, which contains a piece of candy—a succession of little treasures for a precious tot.

Pirate Ship

1. The pirate ship and its appliqués are placed on a grid (1 square = 1 inch). Enlarge the ship and the appliqués on separate grids to establish individual patterns. Cut out the patterns.

2. Use the ship pattern to cut two shapes from **light blue felt**.

3. Cut two of each appliqué, one set for each ship shape. The sails are cut from either **white or black felt**. The flag is cut in **contrasting colors** of the sails. The hull is **brown** and the remaining appliqués are cut from **appropriate felt colors**.

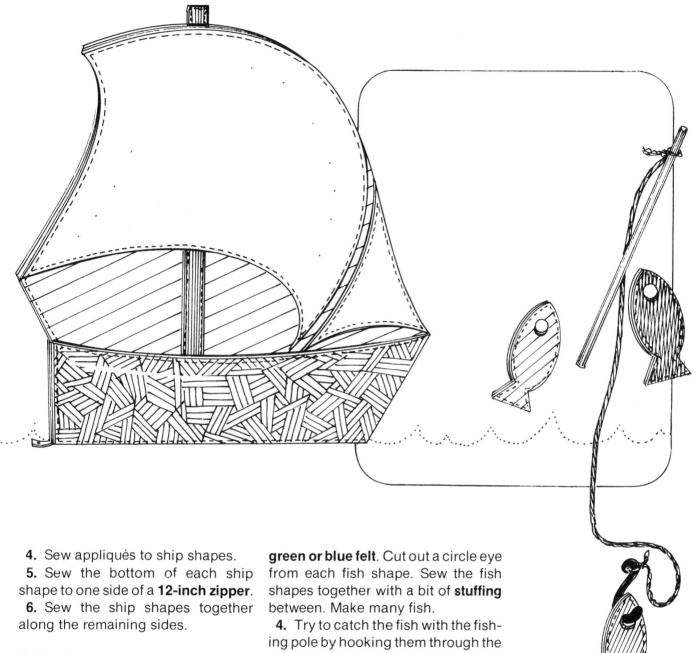

4. Sew appliqués to ship shapes.

5. Sew the bottom of each ship shape to one side of a **12-inch zipper**.

6. Sew the ship shapes together along the remaining sides.

Sailboat

1. The pattern for the sailboat is the same as the pirate ship, but the sails are different. Construct the sailboat as you did the pirate ship.

2. Tie one end of a length of string to a **short wooden dowel** and the other end to a **plastic shower curtain hook**, for a fishing pole and hook.

3. Cut two fish shapes from **light green or blue felt**. Cut out a circle eye from each fish shape. Sew the fish shapes together with a bit of **stuffing** between. Make many fish.

4. Try to catch the fish with the fishing pole by hooking them through the eye hole. Zip the fish and fishing pole inside the sailboat when not in use.

Treasure

1. The trunk is constructed of two 6½-by-8-inch **brown felt** rectangles, with the two top corners rounded.

2. Glue or sew on the slat and lock appliqués.

3. Sew the bottom of each trunk

shape to one side of a **6-inch zipper**.

4. Sew the trunk shapes together along the remaining sides.

5. Construct the chest of two 4-inch **yellow felt** squares. Glue a lock appliqué to one square.

6. Sew the trunk shapes together along three sides.

7. Tuck a special treasure into the chest. Zip the chest into the trunk and slip the trunk into the ship.

1 square = 1 inch

All Aboard the Train to Adventure

Chug Chug, Choo Choo, and it's off to the country.

During the 1800s and up into the 1930s, traveling by train was the chic mode of transportation, being faster and more tolerable than the horse and buggy. It was also the setting for many a romantic and mystery novel, with plots that endeared heros and heroines to the heart and challenged the mind. Today the jet plane has almost replaced the Old Number 9s, as the great railroads are slowly joining the ranks of the Conestoga wagon and the Stanley Steamer. Your little ones may never experience the *clickety clack* of the wheels ironing the rails and the quaint sights that rush by, but with this choo choo, a train ride to a new adventure departs every day.

Locomotive, Caboose, And Coal Car

1. The locomotive and the caboose are placed on a grid (1 square = 1 inch). Enlarge the grid and the designs on paper to establish your patterns. Cut out the patterns.

2. Use the patterns to cut out two locomotives from **black felt** and two cabooses from **red felt**. Cut out two roof shapes from **another color felt** for the locomotive.

3. Draw a 3½-by-5-inch rectangle on paper for the coal car. Add a 1-inch-square tab on each side of the rectangle, 1 inch from the bottom. The tabs will be used to connect the cars.

4. Use the pattern to cut two coal

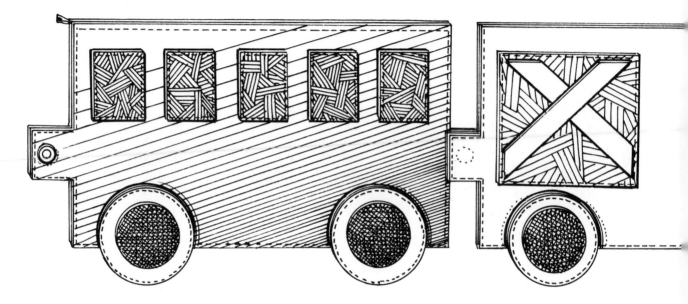

car shapes from **black felt**.

5. Cut windows, bells, cowcatchers, boilers, roof shingles, puffs of smoke, and a pile of coal from **assorted colors of felt**. Sew or glue all appliqués in their places, except the coal and the smoke.

6. Sew matching locomotive, caboose, and coal car shapes together, with a bit of **stuffing** between each pair. Tuck the smoke and the pile of coal into their proper seams as you sew.

7. For the wheels of each train car, cut eight 2-inch circles from **white felt** and four 1-inch circles from **black or gray felt**.

8. Sew pairs of white circles together with a bit of stuffing between them.

9. Sew one half of a **large sewing snap** to one side of each wheel, and a gray circle to the other side.

10. Sew the remaining halves of the snaps to both sides of each car, near the bottom edge.

11. Snap the wheels in place.

12. Sew halves of sewing snaps to the tabs of the cars (for connecting the cars).

Box And Pullman Cars

1. Draw a 4½-by-8-inch rectangle on paper. Add a 1-inch tab to both sides, 1 inch from the bottom. Cut out designs to establish your pattern.

2. Use the pattern to cut two car shapes for each box or Pullman car you wish to make. You can mix and match **colors of felt**.

3. Cut windows for the pullman car and/or doors for the box cars from **compatible colors of felt**.

4. Sew the windows and/or doors to the car shapes.

5. Sew matching car shapes together along the sides and bottom, leaving the top edge open. If you wish, sew a **6-inch zipper** to the top of the car, or simply sew edges closed.

6. Make and snap on wheels, as directed above.

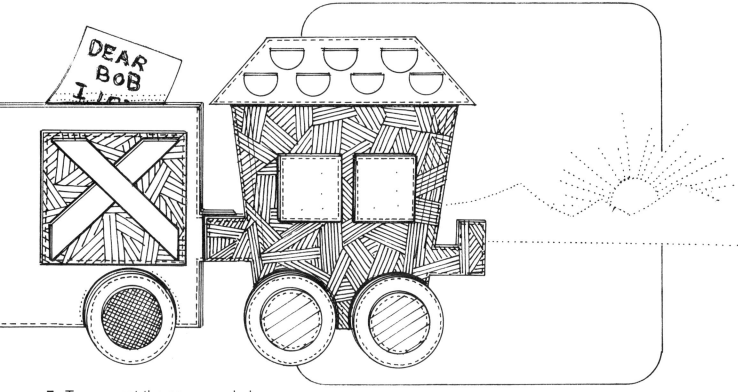

7. To connect the cars, sew halves of sewing snaps to the tabs and snap tabs together.

1 square = 1 inch

A School Bus With a Special Surprise

*Going to school will be
fun every time your
little ones take the bus.*

Do your children take a bus to school? Whether they do or not, here is a felt school bus that they will want to take every day of the week. Inside it can be zipped pens, pencils, and erasers. Also tucked away is a miniature lunch box that is conveniently the right size for a chocolate chip cookie or two. Who knows? With this school bus, your scholastic wizards might never miss a day of lessons.

School Bus

1. The passenger section of the bus is a 6½-by-12-inch rectangle with the top left corner rounded. The front motor section is a 2-by-4-inch rectangle, with the top slanted down slightly. Draw both rectangles on paper to establish your pattern. Cut out the pattern.

2. Use the pattern to cut two bus shapes from **blue felt**.

3. Trace the letters from the book onto tracing paper to spell out the name of your child's school. Cut out the letters for your patterns.

4. Use the letter patterns to cut letters from **any color felt**. Glue or sew them to a long felt strip.

5. Sew the school sign to one bus shape, 2 inches from the bottom.

6. Cut two grills from **white or gray felt** and sew one to the lower front of each bus shape.

7. Cut two 2-by-10-inch rectangles from a **clear plastic** (sold by the yard at dime stores).

8. Sew a plastic rectangle to each bus shape, along the sides and bottom edge. Sew widthwise across the plastic, forming 2-inch-square pockets.

9. Sew the backside of each bus shape to one side of a **6-inch zipper**.
10. Sew the bus shapes together along the remaining sides.
11. Cut eight 2½-inch circles from **black felt** for the tires and four 1-inch circles from **gray felt** for the hubcaps.
12. Sew every two black circles together with a bit of **stuffing** between them.
13. Sew one half of a **large sewing snap** to one side of each tire and a hubcap to the other side.
14. Sew the matching halves of the snaps to each side of the bus, near the bottom edge.
15. Snap on the tires.

Schoolchildren

1. Cut two 1½-inch circles from **skin-tone pieces of felt** for each head and bus driver. There should be nine children's heads.

2. Sew matching circles together with a bit of stuffing between each.

3. Glue simple facial features to one side of each head.

4. Place one smiling face into each plastic pocket.

Lunch Box

1. Cut two 3¼-inch squares from **any color felt**.

2. Place the two squares on top of each other and round the two top corners. Also cut an opening into both shapes to form a handle.

3. Sew along the sides and the bottom of the two shapes to form the lunch box.

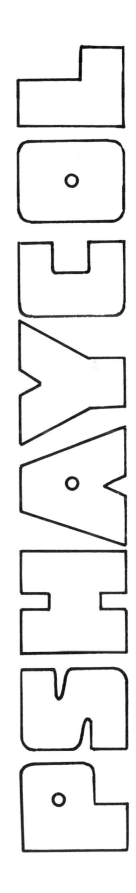

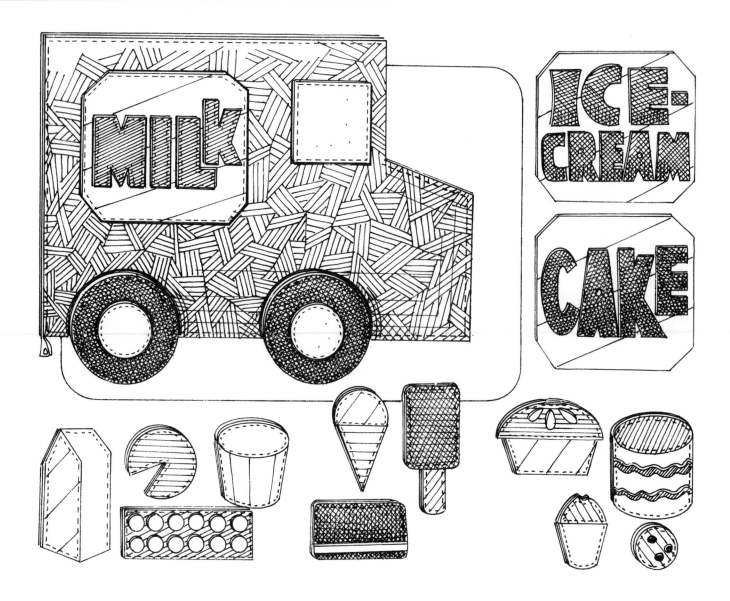

A Delivery Truck Comes to Your Neighborhood

It's time to load the truck and start delivering the merchandise.

Old timers talk about the days when food was fresher, cost less, and was delivered to the front door. With scarcity of local farms and the advent of the large shopping center, practically "around the corner" in every large city, home delivery of foods and goods is a thing of the past. Here and there you might still observe an occasional dairy truck delivering milk and eggs before breakfast, or a laundry service dropping off sheets and towels before bedtime, but these times are rare.

Make a fleet of delivery trucks so that your children can experience a time gone by, when courteous, front-door service was a way of life.

Delivery Truck
1. The body of the delivery truck is a rectangle 6½ inches tall and 7½ inches long. The hood section is a 3½-by-2-inch rectangle, with the top angled slightly. Draw both rectangles on paper, butting each other, to establish your pattern. Cut out the pattern, then angle the hood.

2. Use the pattern to cut two truck shapes from **colors of felt**.

3. Cut two 3½-inch **bright color felt** squares for the signs on the truck. Snip off the corners. Now you need letters that spell out the type of truck you are making: cut them freehand.

4. Glue the letters to both signs.

5. Cut out two windows, in **compatible colors of felt**.

6. Sew or glue a sign and a window to each truck shape.

7. Sew the backs of the truck shapes to a **6-inch zipper**.

8. Sew the truck shapes together along the remaining sides.

9. Cut eight 2-inch circles from **black felt** for the tires, and four ¾-inch circles from **gray felt** for the hubcaps.

10. Sew every two black circles together with a bit of **stuffing** between them.

11. Sew one half of a **large sewing snap** to the center of one side of each tire. Glue or sew a gray circle to the other side.

12. Sew the matching halves of the snaps to both sides of the truck, near the bottom edge.

13. Snap on the wheels.

Fresh Foods

1. You can trace some foods directly from the drawing. Others you can create yourself. Trace the foods from the book onto tracing paper to establish your patterns. Cut out the patterns.

2. Use the patterns to cut two of each shape, along with the appliqués, from **appropriate colors of felt**.

3. Sew the appliqués to the food shapes before sewing matching shapes together, with a bit of stuffing between each.

4. Zip the foods into the truck.

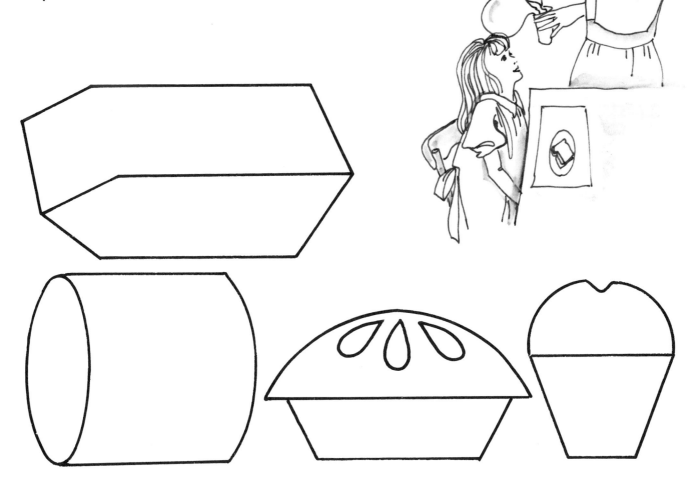

A Firetruck for Hours of Hot Fun

Someday you just may have a firefighter in the family.

One popular childhood aspiration is to be a firefighter. Children somehow see this heroic figure as a modern-day swashbuckler, one who fights his way into a burning building and rescues trapped people. What young ones do not see is the dull chores on one side of the spectrum and the hazardous working conditions on the other. Adults cannot stress enough the potential dangers of fire and playing with matches. This firetruck will familiarize children with firefighting equipment and help them extinguish only imaginary blazes.

Firetruck

1. The firetruck is placed on a grid (1 square = ½ inch). Enlarge the grid and the designs on paper to establish your pattern. Cut out the pattern.

2. Use the pattern to cut two firetruck shapes from **red felt**.

3. Cut eight 2-inch circles from **black felt** for the firetruck's tires. Cut four 1-inch circles from **gray felt** for the hubcaps.

4. The ladder, bell, window, axe, bumper, and fire extinguisher are also on the grid. Make individual patterns by enlarging the grid or draw

them freehand on paper.

5. Cut four ladder shapes from **brown felt**.

6. Sew every two ladder shapes together to form two ladders.

7. Cut two bells, windows, axes, bumpers, and fire extinguishers from **assorted colors of felt**.

8. Construct the bell, axe, and fire extinguisher by sewing matching shapes together.

9. Sew or glue a bumper and a window to each firetruck shape.

10. Sew the tops of the main part of the two firetruck shapes to a **6-inch zipper**.

11. Sew the firetruck shapes together along the remaining sides.

12. Sew every two black circles together with a bit of **stuffing** between them to make tires.

13. Sew one half of a **large sewing snap** to the center of one side of each tire. Sew a gray circle to the other side.

14. Sew the matching halves of the snaps to sides of the firetruck, near the bottom edges.

15. Snap on the tires.

16. Sew halves of snaps to the axe, bell, fire extinguisher, and both ends of each ladder. For the fire extinguisher, make a yarn hose with a felt nozzle and tuck it into the seam.

17. Sew the matching halves of the snaps to the sides of the firetruck. Snap the equipment in place.

18. Sew the end of the hose, opposite the nozzle, inside the firetruck. Gather the yarn hose neatly and zip it inside the truck.

1 square = ½ inch

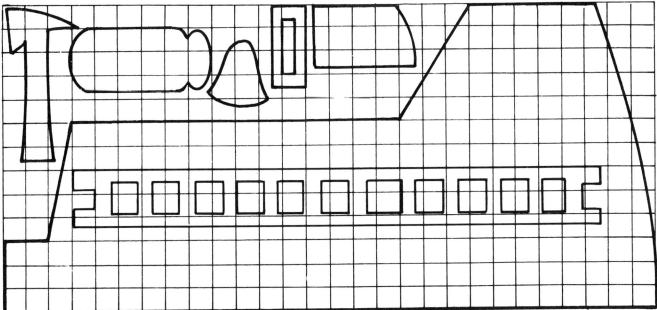

Journey to the Stars in a Rocket Ship

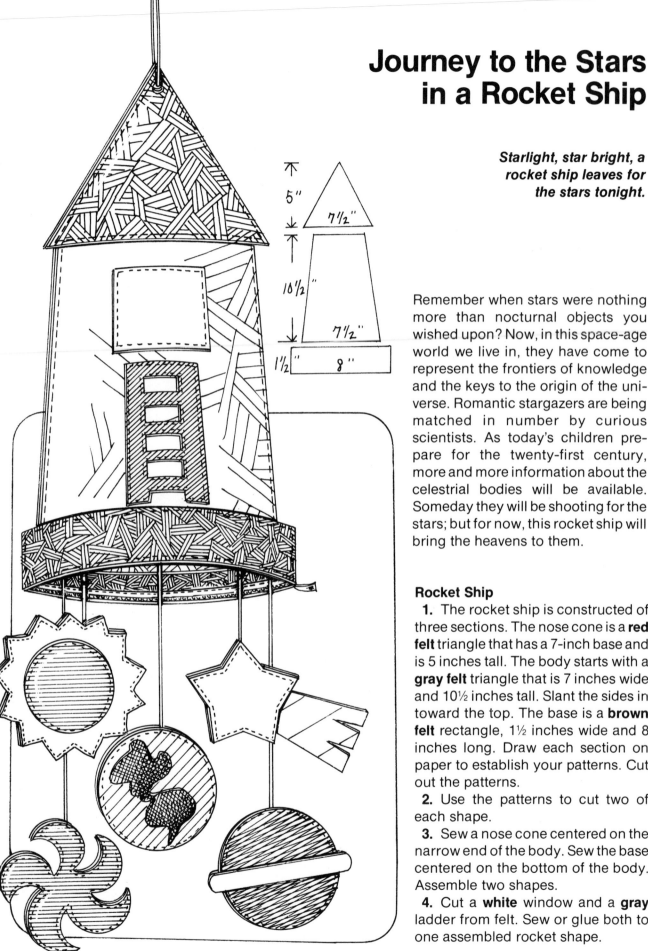

5"

7½"

10½"

7½"

1½"   8"

Starlight, star bright, a rocket ship leaves for the stars tonight.

Remember when stars were nothing more than nocturnal objects you wished upon? Now, in this space-age world we live in, they have come to represent the frontiers of knowledge and the keys to the origin of the universe. Romantic stargazers are being matched in number by curious scientists. As today's children prepare for the twenty-first century, more and more information about the celestrial bodies will be available. Someday they will be shooting for the stars; but for now, this rocket ship will bring the heavens to them.

Rocket Ship

1. The rocket ship is constructed of three sections. The nose cone is a **red felt** triangle that has a 7-inch base and is 5 inches tall. The body starts with a **gray felt** triangle that is 7 inches wide and 10½ inches tall. Slant the sides in toward the top. The base is a **brown felt** rectangle, 1½ inches wide and 8 inches long. Draw each section on paper to establish your patterns. Cut out the patterns.

2. Use the patterns to cut two of each shape.

3. Sew a nose cone centered on the narrow end of the body. Sew the base centered on the bottom of the body. Assemble two shapes.

4. Cut a **white** window and a **gray** ladder from felt. Sew or glue both to one assembled rocket shape.

5. Sew the bottom of each assembled rocket shape to one side of a **6-inch zipper**.

6. Sew the rocket shapes together along the remaining sides.

Heavenly Bodies

1. The patterns for the whirling galaxy, shooting star, and sun can be traced directly from the drawing. The other planets are 3½-inch circles.

2. Use the patterns to cut two of each shape from **appropriate colors of felt**. Also cut out appliqués for the earth, saturn, and the sun.

3. Sew or glue the appliqués to their corresponding shapes.

4. Sew matching shapes together with a bit of **stuffing** between each.

5. Poke a hole into the top of each heavenly body. Tie one end of a **length of cord or yarn** into each hole.

6. Sew the other end of each length of cord or yarn to the inside of the rocket.

7. The rocket ship can hang as a mobile or can be played with on a flat surface. Zip the heavenly bodies into the rocket ship when not in use.

Drift Along in a Hot-Air Balloon

A message from Mom, in a hot-air balloon, will bring your little one back to earth.

People are attracted to hot-air ballooning, as it affords them the luxury of rising above the noise and confusion of life and offers a sense of adventure by letting the wind be the navigator. Most children would love such a lofty experience, and this hot-air balloon can let their imaginations soar. And it is a great place to leave a message when they have to come down to earth.

Balloon

1. Draw a large oval, with one end tapered, on paper to establish your pattern. Cut out the pattern.

2. Use the pattern to cut two balloon shapes from **white or a bright-colored felt**.

3. Place the two shapes together, right sides facing, and sew around the curved edge, leaving the tapered end unsewn.

4. Turn inside out and **stuff** the balloon firmly.

5. Sew the tapered end closed.

6. Draw fanciful designs on the balloon with **felt-tip markers**.

7. For the gondola, cut two same-size rectangles from **a compatible color fabric or felt**. Sew them together along the sides and bottom.

8. Tie three identical long **lengths of yarn** together at their centers, with a fourth long length of yarn passing through the knot. The fourth length will be for hanging.

9. Sew the knotted center of the lengths of yarn to the top of the balloon.

10. Drape the lengths of yarn evenly over the balloon and secure in place with a few stitches.

11. Sew the ends of the lengths of yarn, evenly spaced, inside the top of the gondola.

4

NURSERY RHYMES

How quickly the innocence of youth surrenders to the complexities of adulthood. Childhood lasts but a fleeting moment, as toys are replaced with the tools of the trade. But nursery rhymes, like pleasant childhood memories, are never forgotten.

Mother Goose and Her Fluffy Gander

Everyone needs a trusting friend, and for Mother Goose it is her fluffy white gander.

Through the years, Mother Goose has become the curator of some of the best-loved nursery rhymes. In fact, she is the principal character.

*Old Mother Goose, when
She wanted to wander,
Would ride through the air
On a very fine gander.*

*Mother Goose had a house,
'Twas built in a wood,
Where an owl at the door
For a sentinel stood.*

Mother Goose

1. Mother Goose and her gander are placed on a grid (1 square = ¾ inch). Enlarge the grid and the designs on paper to establish your patterns. Cut out the patterns.

2. Use the patterns to cut two heads, four hands, and four legs from a **skin-tone fabric**. Cut two bodices and four arms from **blue fabric**.

3. Sew a hand to each arm.

4. Sew two legs to the bottom of each bodice and a head to the top.

5. Place the two assembled doll shapes together, right sides facing, and sew around all edges, leaving a bit of side seam unsewn.

6. Turn the doll inside out, **stuff** firmly, and hand-stitch the open seam closed.

7. Embroider facial features on the head or draw them on with **indelible felt-tip markers**.

8. Sew on **white or gray yarn** hair.

9. Hem and gather a piece of **blue print fabric**, large enough to fit around the doll's waist, for the skirt.

10. Sew the skirt to the doll.

11. Cut a large apron and a pocket from **white felt**.

12. Sew the pocket to the bottom of the apron.

13. Center a length of **white ribbon** along the top of the apron and sew it in place.

14. Tie the apron around the doll's waist.

15. Roll a piece of **blue fabric** into a cone and trim the open end so that it fits onto the doll's head. Glue the fabric into a cone shape. Sew the cone to a **blue felt** ring that has been cut to size for the hat's brim.

16. Place the hat on Mother Goose's head.

The Gander

1. Use your patterns to cut two bird shapes and two wing shapes from **white felt**. Cut one feet shape from **orange felt**.

2. Sew a wing, a beak, and a black button eye to each bird shape.

3. Sew the two bird shapes together with a bit of stuffing between them. Tuck the feet between the shapes as you sew.

4. Slip the goose into Mother Goose's apron pocket.

1 square = ¾ inch

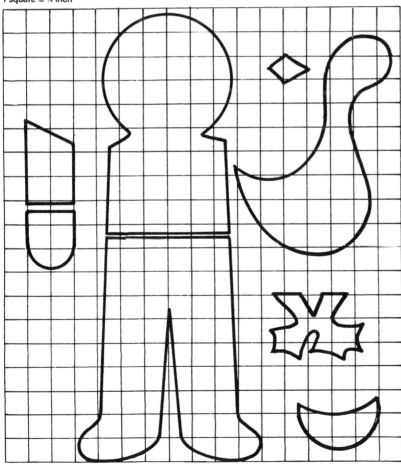

Three Blind Mice, See How They Run

Look near a wedge of cheese to find a trio of adorable mice.

It just may be safer for these three blind mice to be playing with your children in their room than to be running from the farmer's wife in the country. Their tails are safe as long as they don't stray too far from their cozy wedge of cheese.

Three blind mice, three blind mice.
See how they run, see how they run.
They all ran after the farmer's wife.
She cut off their tails with a carving knife.
Did you ever see such a sight in your life,
As three blind mice.

Mice

1. The mice are placed on a grid (1 square = ¾ inch). Enlarge the grid and the designs on paper to establish your patterns. Cut out the patterns.

2. Use the patterns to cut two body shapes from **white felt**, two from **gray felt**, and two from **brown felt**; each mouse will be a different color. Cut out one tail for each mouse, plus two arms for the profile mouse. (Match your colors.) Each front-view mouse has a pink tummy. Cut out five ear middles from **pink felt**.

3. Sew an ear middle to each ear.

4. For each face, cut a pair of eye-glasses from **black felt** and a nose from **pink felt**. Sew or glue everything in place.

5. Sew an arm to each profile mouse shape, and a tummy to two front-view mouse shapes.

6. Place matching body shapes together and sew along the edge, tucking each tail into the seam. Leave a bit of seam unsewn on each mouse.

7. Stuff the mice and sew the open seams closed.

Wedge of Cheese

1. Draw an 8-by-15-inch rectangle on paper. Add a triangle to the top of the rectangle, with one side measuring 8½ inches and another 15 inches. Cut out the rectangle and the triangle separately to establish your patterns.

2. Use the patterns to cut two rectangles from **yellow felt** and two triangles from **white felt**.

3. Sew a triangle to each rectangle along the 15-inch sides.

4. Cut out assorted-size circles and ovals from **yellow and white felt.**

5. Scatter contrasting colors of circles and ovals on one side of each assembled cheese shape, and sew in place.

6. Sew the 8½-inch sides of the top of the cheese shapes to an **8-inch zipper**.

7. Sew the remaining sides of the shapes together to form the wedge of cheese.

1 square = ¾ inch

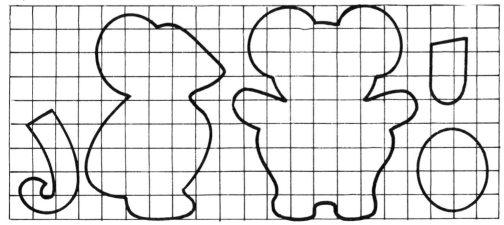

Humpty Dumpty Sat on a Wall

It will take but a gentle lift from tiny hands to put this Humpty Dumpty back on his wall.

One of the important lessons of life we teach growing children is to get back on their feet after an emotional, physical, or psychological fall. As this nursery rhyme recounts, Humpty Dumpty was beyond help; but this doll needs very little effort to get back on his wall.

Humpty Dumpty sat on a wall,
Humpty Dumpty had a great fall.
All the king's horses, and all the king's men,
Couldn't put Humpty together again.

Humpty Dumpty

1. The pattern for Humpty Dumpty is a 7-by-8-inch oval. To make an accurate pattern, fold a piece of paper in half twice, dividing it into four quarters. Draw a curved line on the folded paper, starting 4 inches above from the folded corner and extending to 3½ inches along the bottom edge. Cut out along the curved line.

2. Cut the paper oval in half widthwise. Use the patterns to cut two **blue felt** and two **white felt** half-ovals.

3. Sew a white half-oval to each blue half-oval.

4. Cut out two eyes, a nose, and two **pink** cheeks for each white half-oval. Sew or glue them in place.

5. Embroider a happy grin on one white half-oval and a sad grin on the other.

6. From **black felt**, cut out and sew a crack for the sad face.

7. Sew a **black felt or ribbon** belt across the center of each constructed oval. Sew a **yellow felt** buckle, centered, on each belt.

8. Cut two simple arms and two legs from white felt. Cut out four **colored felt** shoes.

9. Sew two shoes to each leg. You can, if you wish, sew **red felt or ribbon** strips across the legs to give the appearance of striped stockings.

10. Place the two ovals together, right sides out. Tuck the arms and legs into the seam and pin in place.

11. Sew the two ovals together, leaving a bit of seam unsewn.

12. **Stuff** Humpty Dumpty and sew the open seam closed.

Wall

1. Cut two 8-by-12½-inch rectangles from **white or gray felt**.

2. Sew **red felt** bricks, scattered, on each rectangle.

3. Sew one length of each rectangle to one side of a **12-inch zipper**.

4. Sew the remaining sides of the rectangles together to form the wall.

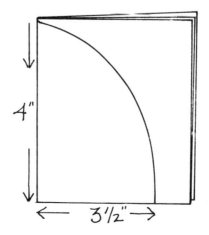

4"

3½"

The Owl and the Pussycat Went to Sea

After a grueling sea adventure, the owl and the pussycat head for your home.

These two unlikely shipmates are looking for a home port, and your children's bedroom looks like a good place to drop anchor. Oh, the stories they can share for those who have creative imaginations. Before you know it, the owl and the pussycat will have your little ones riding the waves to new adventures.

The owl and the pussycat went to sea
In a beautiful pea green boat.
They took some honey, and plenty of money
Wrapped up in a five-pound note.

Owl and Pussycat

1. The owl and the pussycat are placed on a grid (1 square = ¾ inch). Enlarge the grid and the designs on paper to establish your patterns. Cut out the patterns.

2. Use the patterns to cut two body shapes for each animal from **any color felt**. Cut two feet, eyes, cheeks, inner ears, and three feathers from **assorted felt colors**. Also cut out one crown feather, a tail, a nose, a beak, and a mouth.

3. Sew or glue the owl's features to

one body shape.

4. Sew or glue the cat's features to one body shape.

5. Place every two matching body shapes together. Tuck the cat's tail into the seam.

6. Sew matching shapes together, leaving a bit of seam unsewn on each animal.

7. **Stuff** each animal and sew the open seams closed.

8. Tie a **ribbon** around the cat's neck.

Sailboat

1. Draw a semicircle on paper that is 6 inches high at the center and 14 inches long. Add a triangle, with a center height of 10 inches, on top of the straight side of the semicircle.

2. Use the pattern to cut two boat shapes from **brown felt**.

3. From **white felt**, cut two sails that will fit on the triangular section of the boat shapes. There should be a space between the sails so that the exposed brown felt creates the illusion of a mast.

4. Sew the sails to one boat shape.

5. Cut out an anchor and sew it to the boat shape, under the sails.

6. Cut a circle from **yellow felt** and a larger circle from **orange felt**. Cut a pointed design into the edge of the orange circle.

7. Sew the smaller circle, centered, to the larger circle. Add a happy sun face.

8. Sew the left side of each triangular section of the boat shapes to one side of a **10-inch zipper**, tucking a small, **red felt** flag into the seam.

9. Sew the boat shapes together along the remaining sides, tucking the sun into the right top seam.

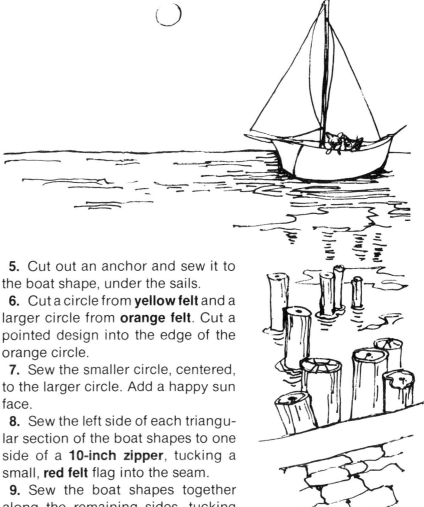

1 square = ¾ inch

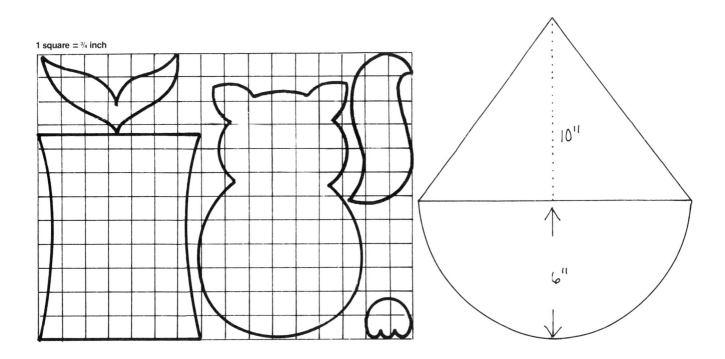

10"

6"

Four and Twenty Blackbirds in a Pie

Won't your little ones have the surprise of their lives when they see how many birds live in this simple pie?

Anyone would be surprised to see just one blackbird fly out of a pie, not to mention what the reaction would be to an entire flock. Darling starlings are the main ingredient in this charming toy, and they will be fun fare for the little kings and queens in your home. This pie will be the dessert to your youngsters' day.

*Sing a song of sixpence,
A pocket full of rye;
Four and twenty blackbirds,
Baked in a pie.*

*When the pie was opened,
The birds began to sing;
Wasn't that a dandy dish
To set before the King?*

Pie

1. Cut two 12½-inch circles from **light brown felt**. Cut one circle in half.

2. Cut several teardrop shapes from **dark brown felt**.

3. Sew the teardrop shapes to both semicircles, in a curved line, passing over the center of the straight sides.

4. Sew the straight sides of the semicircles to a **12-inch zipper.**

5. Sew the circles together.

6. For a pie that will hold a large flock of blackbirds, use a 14½- or a 16½-inch circle.

Blackbirds

1. Trace the blackbird patterns from the book onto tracing paper. Cut out the patterns.

2. Use the patterns to cut two bird shapes from **black felt** and two wing shapes from **gray or black felt**. Also cut out an **orange** beak and two **white** eyes.

3. Sew a wing to one bird shape.

4. Sew or glue two eyes and a beak to a bird shape whose head will face forward. Sew an eye on each bird shape that will face sideways (the beak will be sewn into the seam later).

5. Place the two bird shapes together. Tuck the remaining wing and the beak (if the bird faces sideways) between the shapes.

6. Sew the two shapes together with a bit of **stuffing** between them.

7. Make "four and twenty" blackbirds, or as many as you wish.

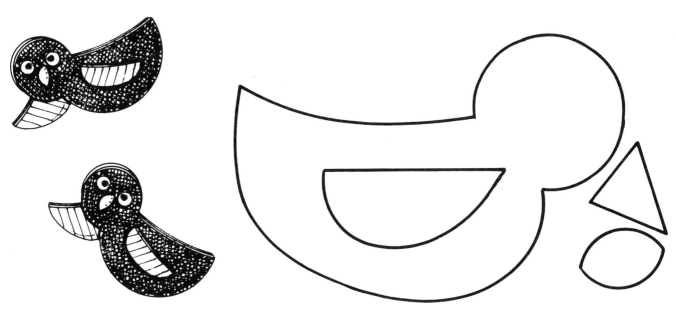

There was an Old Woman Who Lived in a Shoe

Prepare your little babysitters: there are a lot of children living in this shoe.

Having one child around the home can be quite trying, but imagine what life would be like if there were three in every room! Caring for them would most certainly be a labor of love, but the old woman in this nursery rhyme had a stern policy of discipline, as you will see. No one got away with anything, as she ran a tight shoe.

There was an old woman who lived in a shoe,
She had so many children she didn't
know what to do;
She gave them some broth without any bread;
She spanked them all soundly and put
them to bed.

Family

1. The old woman and her children are placed on a grid (1 square = 1 inch). Enlarge the grid and the designs on paper to establish your patterns. Cut out the patterns.

2. Use the patterns to cut two heads, two bodies, four sleeves, two shoes, and two hands for each boy, girl, and the old woman, from **appropriate colors of felt**.

3. The basic patterns can undergo many variations—as the costumes illustrate in the drawings—with the addition of bibs, collars, front yokes, etc. Sew a sleeve to both sides of each clothing shape.

4. For each intended doll, decorate a head with **felt** facial features, **felt or yarn** hair, and hats or ponytails. Decorate the corresponding circles for the heads with hair designs.

5. Sew matching head shapes together with a bit of **stuffing** between them.

6. Place matching body shapes together. Tuck a head, two hands, and two shoes between the shapes, in their proper places.

7. Sew the body shapes together, leaving a bit of the seam unsewn. **Stuff** the dolls and sew the open seams closed.

8. The old woman's bonnet is constructed by sewing **elastic tape** around the edge of a **white fabric** circle. Pull the tape as you sew, gathering the entire edge of the circle.

Shoe House

1. The shoe and its roof are placed on a grid (1 square = 1 inch). Enlarge the grid and the designs on paper to establish your patterns. Cut out the patterns.

2. Use the patterns to cut two shoe shapes from **brown felt** and two roof shapes from **red felt**.

3. From **colored felt** cut a buckle, windows, shutters, crosses for shoelaces, and a door.

4. Sew windows and shutters to both shoe shapes. Sew the buckle, shoelaces, and door to one shape.

5. Sew a roof shape to each shoe shape, with the tongue of each roof shape overlapping its shoe shape.

6. Sew the top edge of each roof shape to one side of a **10-inch zipper**.

7. Sew the shoe house together along the remaining sides.

1 square = 1 inch

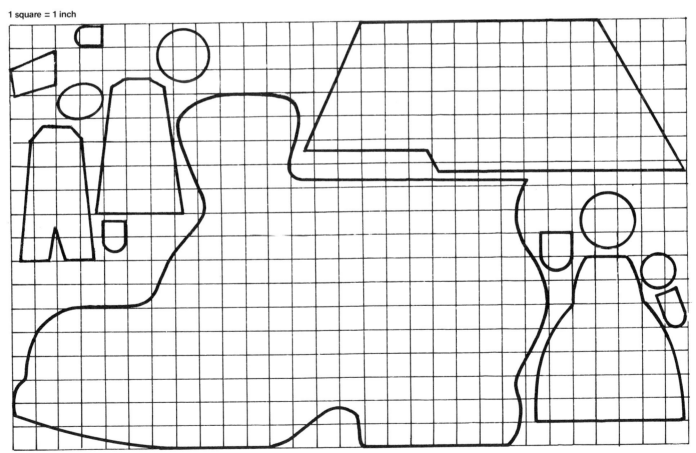

Mistress Mary's Garden

The gal with the green thumb has more than silver bells growing in her garden.

It seems that anything Mistress Mary plants in her garden grows well. Her nursery rhyme, however, doesn't make mention of any fruits or vegetables. Here's a delightful toy that will yield a bushel of fun for your children.

Mary, Mary, quite contrary,
How does your garden grow?
With silver bells and cockle shells,
And pretty maids all in a row.

Mistress Mary

1. Mary, her dress, and the garden tools are placed on a grid (1 square = ½ inch). Enlarge the grid and the designs on paper to establish your patterns. Cut out the patterns.

2. Use the patterns to cut two body shapes from a **skin-tone felt** and two dress shapes from any **color of felt**.

3. Cut out and glue or sew a face on one body shape. Glue or sew a shoe on both feet of each shape.

4. Sew the body shapes together with a bit of **stuffing** between them. Tuck two pigtails into the seam of the head.

5. Sew the dress shapes together along the shoulders and the sides. Cut a slit into the neck at the back to enable the dress to slip over the head and onto the doll.

6. The cap is a **hemmed fabric circle**, sewn gathered on a small length of **elastic tape**. The apron is a piece of **hemmed fabric** that is gathered along one length.

7. Sew one half of a **sewing snap** to each hand.

8. Use the patterns to cut two watering can, spade, and cultivator shapes from **assorted colors of felt**.

9. Sew matching shapes together with a bit of **stuffing** between them.

10. Sew the other snap halves to the tools so that they snap into Mary's hands.

Garden Folder

1. Cut four 14-by-17-inch rectangles from **light green felt** for the garden folder pages.

2. Cut two 12-inch squares from **brown felt** for the plots of soil. Sew each brown square to a green rectangle near a 14-inch side.

3. Cut picket fence shapes from **white felt** for each plot of soil. Sew the fences along the tops of the squares.

4. Cut out eight 2-inch **white felt** squares and eight ½-inch **black felt** squares. Sew a black square to each white square, centered on one side, to form the seed packets.

5. Cut a tomato, pumpkin, strawberry, and pea pod from **appropriate colors of felt**. Sew one to each seed packet.

6. Cut out four flower shapes with leaves, and sew them to the remaining seed packets.

7. Sew four seed packets, equally spaced to each plot of soil, along the right side. Place flowers together and vegetables together.

8. Sew one half of sewing snaps to the plots of soil. They should be in line with the seed packets, four to a row.

9. Sew a simple garden scene, cut from assorted colors of felt, to a third **green** rectangle for the folder's front cover. The back cover is the fourth **green** rectangle.

10. To construct the folder, sew the front cover to the vegetable garden and the back cover to the flower garden, along all sides. Place the two constructed rectangles on top of each other, gardens facing in, and sew together along the left length. The front cover should be on top.

Produce and Flowers

1. Cut eight shapes for each produce and eight shapes for each flower from assorted **colored felt**.

2. Cut out and glue necessary details to four of each shape.

3. Sew appliquéd shapes to their matching produce or flower shape, with a bit of **stuffing** between them.

4. Sew the remaining matching snap halves to the backs of the produce and flowers.

5. Snap the flowers and produce into their respective rows.

1 square = ½ inch

Rub-a-Dub-Dub, Three Men in a Tub

Make sure the drain stopper is in tightly: this tiny tub is setting sail for destinations unknown.

With a little stretch of the imagination, a bathtub does resemble a boat of sorts. Well, that's what the popular nursery rhyme trio, the butcher, the baker and the candlestick maker, thought. They were surely children at heart as they set sail on the high seas in a wooden tub.

Rub-a-dub-dub, three men in a tub,
And who do you think they be?
The butcher, the baker, the candlestick maker,
And all of them gone to sea.

Butcher, Baker, and Candlestick Maker

1. The butcher, baker, and candlestick maker are placed on a grid (1 square = ½ inch). Enlarge the grid and the designs on paper to establish your patterns. Cut out the patterns.

2. Use the patterns to cut three head shapes from **skin-tone felt**, and three matching back head shapes from **brown felt**. From **colors of felt**, cut four shoe shapes, two body shapes, two hat shapes, and one apron for each doll. The hats and aprons are cut from **white felt**.

3. Cut out brown hair and colored facial features for each skin tone head. Sew or glue them in place. Add a visor to the candlestick maker's head.

4. Sew a face to the neck of a body shape, and a hair shape to a second body shape.

5. Sew two hands and two shoes to each body shape.

6. Place assembled corresponding body shapes together and sew along the sides, leaving a bit of seam unsewn.

7. Stuff the dolls and sew the open seams closed.

8. Construct the butcher's and the baker's hats and place them on their respective heads.

9. Sew a pocket to each apron. Sew a length of **white ribbon** to each side of the aprons.

10. Place an apron on each doll and tie the ribbons into a bow at the back.

11. Sew one half of a **sewing snap** to each hand.

Merchants' Supplies

1. Cut two shapes for each meat, bakery, and candlestick maker's product you intend to make. Add appliqués, if you wish, for details.

2. Sew appliqués in place.

3. Sew matching shapes together, with a bit of **stuffing** between them.

4. Sew matching snap halves to the backs of the products.

5. Store the products by placing them in the aprons' pockets or snapping them onto the merchants' hands.

Washtub

1. Cut two 6-by-10-inch rectangles from brown felt. Slightly slant the 10-inch sides.

2. Sew two ribbon or felt strips across each rectangle.

3. Sew the rectangles along the slanted sides and bottom to form the tub.

1 square = ½ inch

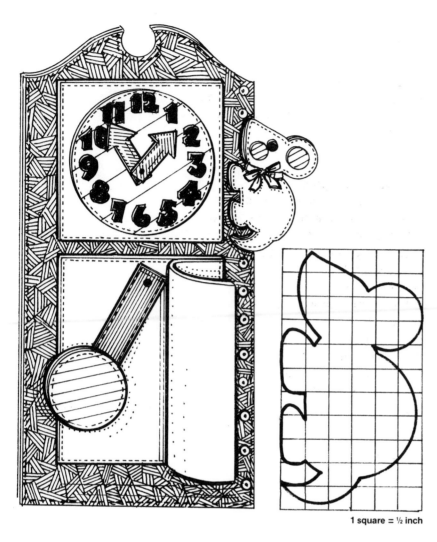

1 square = ½ inch

Hickory Dickory Dock

Here's one cute mouse you will not mind having in your home.

Who knows what prompted the mouse to dash up the clock, but the loud *gong* that signaled the hour must have scared the little fellow to death. Down he went to quieter quarters. This toy will be so much fun for your little ones that every minute of the day will be one o'clock.

> Hickory Dickory Dock
> The mouse ran up the clock:
> The clock struck one
> And down he run
> Hickory Dickory Dock.

Mouse

   1. The mouse is placed on a grid (1 square = ½ inch). Draw the design and the grid on paper to establish your pattern. Cut out the pattern.

   2. Use the pattern to cut two mouse shapes from **white felt**.

   3. Cut out the facial features from **colors of felt**. Sew or glue an eye, a cheek, and an ear middle to each shape.

   4. Sew the mouse shapes together, with a bit of **stuffing** between them.

   5. Tie a ribbon bow around the mouse's neck.

   6. Add half a **sewing snap**, centered, to one side of the body.

Clock

   1. Cut two 10-by-21-inch rectangles from **brown felt**. Round one width of each rectangle and cut a circle into these sides.

   2. Sew a 6½-inch **white felt** square near the rounded end of one clock shape. Sew a 6½-by-8½-inch **white felt** rectangle below the square.

   3. Sew a 5½-inch **yellow felt** circle, centered, on the square.

   4. Cut out numbers for the clock from felt and sew them in place.

   5. For the hands of the clock, cut four arrows. Sew every two arrows together.

   6. Center the hands on the clock face. Thread a button and push the needle through the ends of the square hands and out of the back of the clock. Tie a button to the back. The hands should move freely.

   7. The pendulum is a 3-inch circle sewn to a 1½-by-4½-inch rectangle. Make two pendulum shapes and sew them together.

   8. Attach the pendulum to the rectangle, near the top, in the same way you attached the hands.

   9. Cut out and sew a 6½-by-8½-inch **white felt** door over the pendulum rectangle.

   10. Sew the two clock shapes together, then stuff with **quilt batting**.

   11. Sew many **sewing snap halves** to one side (opposite the half on the mouse) of the clock.

5

FAVORITE FABLES

Little ones do not have to board boats, trains, or airplanes to venture off to exciting places. All they have to do is fire up the wheels of their imaginations, close their eyes for a moment, and travel to such marvelous places as Toyland, Old MacDonald's Farm, and Wonderland, where their favorite fable friends abide. A child's journey of a thousand delights begins with the blink of an eye.

Alice's Wonderful Wonderland

You do not have to tumble down a rabbit hole to relive Alice's adventure.

It is said that dreaming is as important to life as eating and sleeping. Everyone experiences some degree of slumber cinema, from the first days of life to the autumn years. Little children tend to remember the everyday occurrences in pleasant dreams that are, more or less, extensions of their everyday activities. One of the more famous dreamers was a little girl named Alice, who journeyed into a strange land inhabited by a population of mad but lovable characters. Now your young ones can meet the Mad Hatter, the March Hare, and the wacky citizens of Wonderland—all without falling down a rabbit hole.

Alice's Wonderland
1. Cut four 11-by-14½-inch rectangles—two from **light green felt**, one from **light blue felt**, and one from **light gray felt**.
2. Cut a rabbit hole, leaves, and rocks from **assorted felt colors**. Sew the rabbit hole, leaves, and grass to one green rectangle. (The other green rectangle will have no sewn-on appliqués.)

3. Cut a second rabbit hole, serpentine path, floor, shelf, table, door, and appliqués from **colors of felt**. Sew the shapes to the gray rectangle, in a scene.

4. Cut a cloud, sun, trees, ground line, and flowers from **colors of felt**. Sew the shapes to the blue rectangle, in a scene.

5. Place the appliquéd green rectangle on the gray rectangle, right sides facing out.

6. With the green rectangle facing you, sew a **14-inch zipper** to the right sides. Sew the rectangles together along the remaining sides.

7. Place the blue and unappliquéd green rectangle together, right sides facing out.

8. With the blue rectangle facing you, sew a **14-inch zipper** to the right side. Sew the rectangles together along the remaining sides.

9. Sew one half of **large sewing snaps** scattered about the room and garden scenes.

10. Place the two constructed rectangles together, zippered sides in line with each other, and sew together along the sides opposite the zippered side to form a folder.

Alice and Friends

1. The Wonderland characters are placed on a grid (1 square = ½ inch). Enlarge the grid and the designs on paper to establish your patterns. Cut out the patterns.

2. Use the patterns to cut two of each body shape; cut four hands,

arms, and shoes from appropriate **colors of felt**. Clothing accessories, such as bow ties and hearts, require one of each shape. The backs of the Mad Hatter's and the March Hare's jackets are made by placing the two front jacket halves together and cutting out one shape.

3. Construct two complete doll shapes for each character, with heads, arms, shoes, and all other appliqués sewn in place. Profile characters have facial features on both doll shapes. Front-view characters have a face on one shape and a hair-colored head shape on the other.

4. Place matching doll shapes together and sew around all sides of each, leaving a small section of seam on a straight side unsewn.

5. Stuff the dolls and sew the open seams closed.

6. Alice's dress and the White Rabbit's costume are made separately. Sew the apron to a dress shape. Sew the dress shapes together. Cut a small slit in the back of the dress at the neck so the garment will slip over Alice's head. The White Hare's sandwich-board apron is held together with lengths of ribbons attached at the top and sides.

7. Sew on **yarn** hair and whiskers where called for. The King's and Queen's wands are **red felt** hearts glued to short lengths of pipe cleaners.

8. Sew the matching **snap halves** to the backs of the Wonderland characters. Snap them to the inside of the folder.

1 square = ½ inch

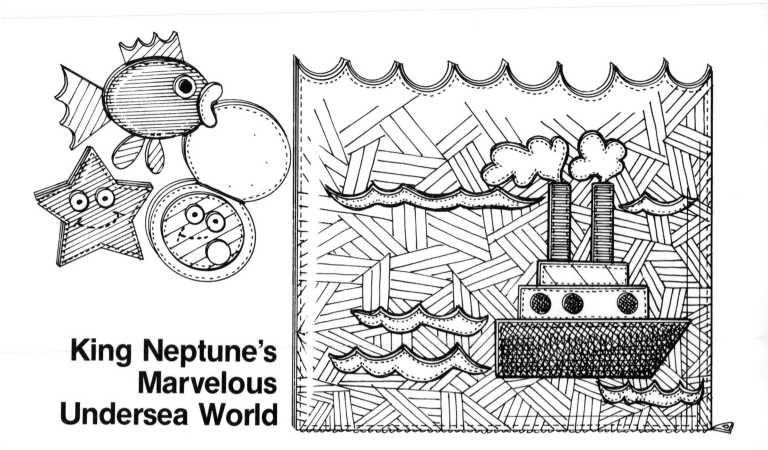

King Neptune's Marvelous Undersea World

The universe below the surface of the ocean is a melting pot of exciting creatures.

King Neptune has been decreed the ruler of the lands and kingdoms of the oceans. With so many denizens of the deep lurking about, he can surely use the volunteer help of your youngsters. Think of the fun they will have playing with the clams, jellyfish, turtles, assorted fish, and, yes, even a mermaid.

Sea

1. Cut two 11-by-14½-inch rectangles from **light blue felt**.

2. Place the rectangles together and cut a scalloped design into one long side of both rectangles.

3. Make a ship from **felt** shapes and waves from **white felt**.

4. Sew the ship and the wave appliqués to one rectangle.

5. Sew the unscalloped lengths of the rectangles to a **14-inch zipper**. Sew the rectangles together along the remaining sides.

Clam, Starfish, Jellyfish, Turtle, and Fish

1. For the clam, cut four 4-by-5-inch ovals from **white felt**, one smaller oval from **pink felt**, and two white eyes and a pearl.

2. Sew or glue the eyes and the pearl on the pink oval. Embroider a smile.

3. Sew the pink oval to a white oval.

4. Sew white ovals together in pairs, with a bit of **stuffing** between.

5. Sew the two stuffed ovals together along a small section of seam, pink oval facing in.

6. Work on the starfish next. Cut two stars from 5-inch **colored felt** circles.

7. Sew or glue on eyes, and embroider a smile on one star.

8. Sew the star shapes together, with a bit of **stuffing** between them.

9. For the jellyfish, cut two 3-by-5-inch semi-ovals from pink felt.

10. Sew eyes along the straight edge of one shape.

11. Sew the two semi-ovals together, with stuffing in between and lengths of **yarn** tucked into the straight sides.

12. For the turtle, cut two 5-by-6-inch ovals from **dark green felt**. Cut four feet, one head, and one tail from **light green felt**. Also cut out a shell design from white felt.

13. Glue the shell design to one oval. Place the two ovals together with the feet, tail and head tucked between the shapes.

14. Sew together with a bit of stuffing between them. Add two eyes to the head.

15. For the fish, cut two 4-by-5-inch ovals from **blue felt**. Also cut out top and bottom fins, tail, eyes, and mouth shapes, from **appropriate colors of felt**.

16. Sew or glue an eye and a mouth shape to each oval.

17. Sew the ovals together, with the tail and fins tucked into place and a bit of **stuffing** between them.

Mermaid and King Neptune

1. The mermaid and King Neptune are placed on a grid (1 square = ½ inch). Enlarge the grid and the designs on paper to establish your patterns. Cut out the patterns.

2. Use the patterns to cut four arms, four feet, and two of each remaining shape from appropriate **colors of felt**.

3. Sew or glue on eyes and embroider a smile on one head of each character.

4. Sew two arms to King Neptune's body and two feet to his skirt. Sew a mermaid's body shape to a fish shape. Construct two complete body shapes for each character.

5. Place matching body shapes together and sew around all edges, leaving a small section of seam unsewn.

6. Stuff each character and sew the open seam closed.

7. Sew **bundles of yarn** on the mermaid's head for hair and add a necklace of **colored felt** flowers around her neck.

8. Sew **yarn** hair to King Neptune's head and top with a crown. Sew a pitchfork to one hand and a pearl to the other.

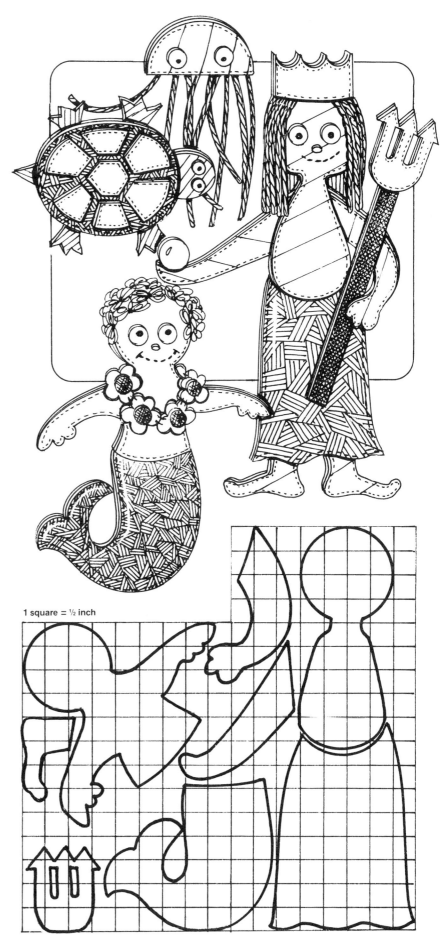

1 square = ½ inch

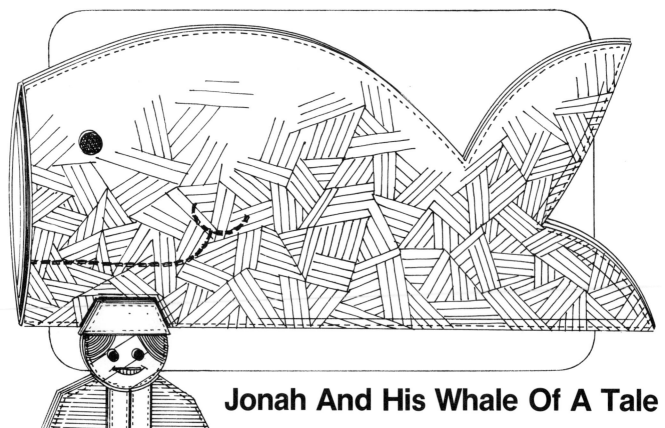

Jonah And His Whale Of A Tale

Jonah was a victim of one of life's important lessons: "Sometimes you eat the fish, and sometimes the fish eats you."

The last thing old Jonah expected while fishing one day was that he would wind up exchanging places with the bait at the end of his fishing pole. It must have been a mighty large whale that mistook him for a tasty

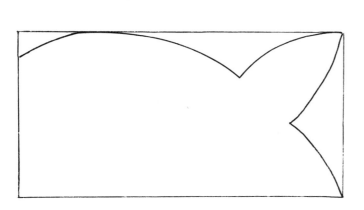

minnow. Fortunately he lived to tell of his harrowing experience, and today it is one of the best-loved Biblical stories among children. With this delightful toy, young adventurous minds can recount this famous parable over and over again.

Whale

1. Draw a 7-by-14-inch rectangle on paper. Draw the whale design inside the rectangle, as shown in the diagram. Cut out the pattern.

2. Use the pattern to cut two whale shapes from **gray or light blue felt**.

3. Sew or glue on an eye and embroider a smile on both whale shapes.

4. Sew the whale shapes together along all sides except the front (the face).

Jonah

1. Jonah is placed on a grid (1 square = ½ inch). Enlarge the grid and the designs on paper to establish your patterns. Cut out the patterns.

2. Use the patterns to cut two robe shapes from **dark blue felt** and one from **white felt**. Cut one blue robe shape in half lengthwise. Cut out two head shapes, one in a **skin tone** and the other in a **hair color**, two hands, two hats, and several fish shapes in **appropriate felt colors**.

3. Cut out strips for robe edging, cuffs, a fishing pole, fish, and a hook from **assorted felt colors**.

4. Sew the edging, hands, cuffs, hook, and fishing pole to the cut robe shapes.

5. Gather together the fish and sew to the white robe shape.

6. Embroider a fishing line on both front robe shapes, and another length of line connecting the fish on the white robe shape.

7. Sew or glue **felt** hair and facial features to the skin-tone head shape. Sew a hat shape to both head shapes.

8. Sew the face to the white robe shape and the hair shape to the uncut blue robe shape.

9. Place the two constructed shapes together and sew along all sides with a bit of **stuffing** between them.

10. Place the cut robe shapes on the constructed body shape and sew them in place along the shoulders and sides.

1 square = ½ inch

Last Call For Noah's Ark

Warning: Occupancy by more than two of each animal on the ark is dangerous.

Noah must have had one heck of a job of not only trying to locate two of each creature on Earth but capturing and feeding them for forty days and forty nights. What a relief it must have been when the water receded! Here's an action toy that has "juvenile fun" written all over it. There's only one problem—how do you say "All

ashore who's going ashore" in elephant or lion talk?

Ark

1. The roof starts with a 3½-by-11-inch rectangle. Cut the side short on a slant so that the top measures 6½ inches. The cabin is a 4-by-11-inch rectangle. The hull is a 7-by-13-inch rectangle, with the top edge curved and the two bottom corners rounded. Draw the three shapes on paper to establish your patterns. Cut out the patterns.

2. Use the patterns to cut two roof shapes from **red felt**, two cabin shapes from **light blue felt**, and two hull shapes from **brown felt**.

3. Cut out small windows for the cabin and a larger window for the roof. Also cut out a **white felt** dove for the roof's window.

4. Sew the dove to the large window and the window to a roof shape. Sew the smaller windows near the top edge of a cabin shape.

5. Sew a roof to a cabin shape and the cabin to a hull shape.

6. Sew the top of each roof to a **6-inch zipper**.

7. Sew the ark together along the remaining sides.

Animals

1. The animals are placed on a grid (1 square = ½ inch). Enlarge the grid and the designs on paper to establish your patterns.

2. Use the patterns to cut two of each animal shape from **appropriate**

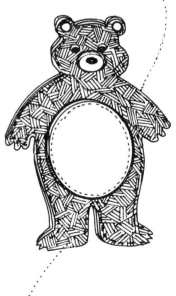

colors of felt. Cut out details, such as ear middles, tummies, stripes, and spots. The lion's mane is shown in dotted lines on the grid.

3. Sew or glue the appliqués to the animal shapes.

4. Place matching animal shapes together. Tuck details, such as the tails and the turtle's feet, between the shapes.

5. Sew the animal shapes together with a bit of **stuffing** between them.

1 square = ½ inch

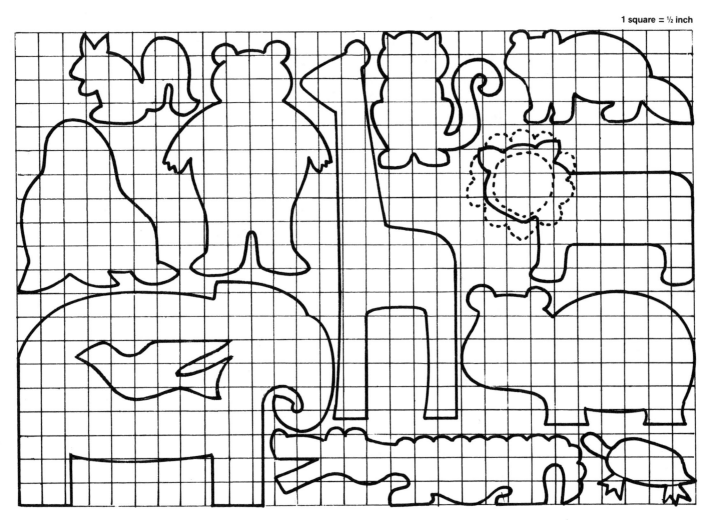

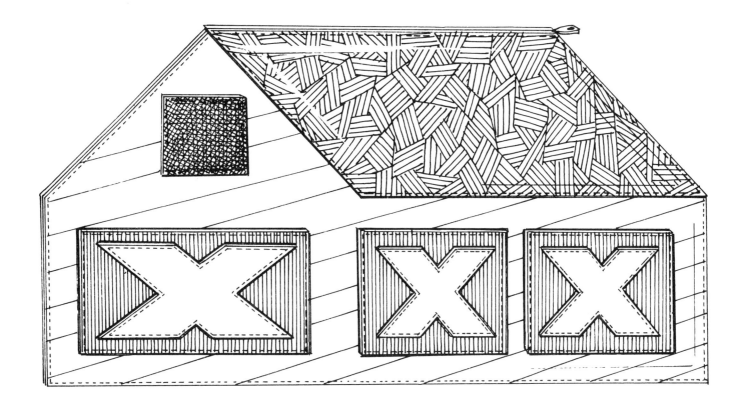

Old MacDonald Had a Farm

Being a farmer is an arduous occupation, especially when more than one animal is being raised.

According to the fairy-tale lore, no one would ever have envied Farmer MacDonald his occupation. Raising cattle alone can be a demanding job, but he took on the responsibility of chickens, pigs, and a host of other noisy animals. All that clucking, mooing, oinking, and baaing must have been music to his ears. Children have a natural affection for animals of all kinds, and to them, Old MacDonald's farm must seem like the house of fun at the amusement park.

Barn

1. The barn is an 8-by-14-inch rectangle with the top corners cut off, so that the top measures 8½ inches. Draw the design on paper to establish your pattern. Cut out the pattern.

2. Use the pattern to cut two barn shapes from white or **gray felt**.

3. Cut off the top section of the paper to create a roof pattern. Study the drawing.

4. Use the roof pattern to cut a roof shape from **red felt**.

5. Cut barn doors from **brown felt**, and X designs and a window from **black felt**.

6. Sew the roof to one barn shape.

7. Sew an X appliqué to each barn door. Sew the doors and the window to the barn shape with the roof.

8. Sew the top of each barn shape to one side of an **8-inch zipper**. Sew the remaining sides of the barn together.

Farm Animals

1. The animals are placed on a grid (1 square = ½ inch). Enlarge the grid

and the designs on paper to establish your patterns. Cut out the patterns.

2. Use the patterns to cut two of each animal shape from **appropriate colors of felt**. Cut out four legs for the sheep and four for the lamb.

3. Cut additional details such as ears, wings, tails, and horns from **colors of felt**. Study the drawing to see which detail goes with which animal.

4. Sew or glue the details on the proper animals.

5. Place matching animal shapes together. Tuck details such as tails, mane, and chicken feet into their proper places between the animal shapes.

6. Sew matching animal shapes together with a bit of **stuffing** between them.

1 square = ½ inch

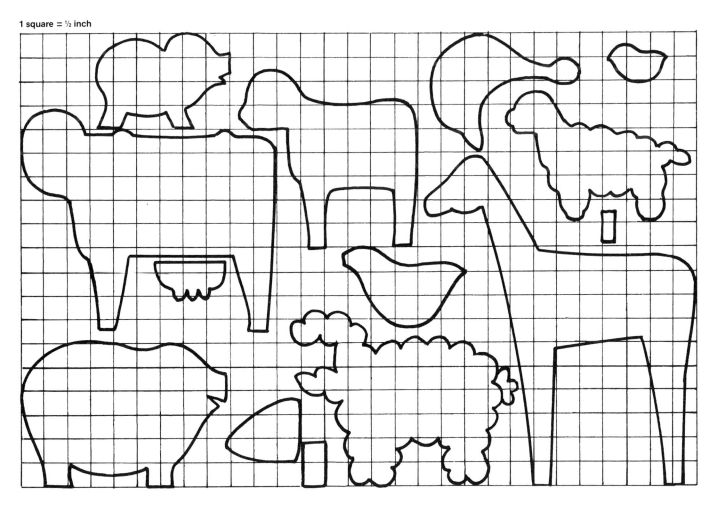

A Babe's Ticket to Toyland

There will be nonstop fun on the streets of Toyland today.

When you go shopping with your children, the toy store is probably the first stop on their list. Think of all those wonderful sights that line the canyons of the store. Here's a perpetual ticket to Toyland, good for any time a youngster is in the mood for fun. This hamlet is filled with some of children's favorite friends, including Jack in the Box and the candy people.

Letter Block

1. Cut two 12½-inch squares from **felt in two different colors**.
2. Cut a large letter A and an apple from **any color felt**.
3. Sew the A to one square and the apple to the other.
4. Sew one side of a **12-inch zipper** to one side of each square. Sew the squares together along the remaining sides.

Toys And Candies

1. The toys and candies are placed on a grid (1 square = ½ inch). Enlarge the grid and the designs on paper to establish your patterns. Cut out the patterns.
2. Use the patterns to cut two of each shape from **appropriate colors of felt**. The lollipop and scoop of ice cream are 3-inch circles. The ice cream cone is a triangle with 3-inch base and a center height of 3½ inches. The lollipop and ice-pop sticks are 1-by-3½-inch rectangles rounded at one end. Cut out assorted hands.
3. Cut out and glue or sew facial features on one shape of each doll and candy. Embroider additional features. Sew on the bear's tummy.
4. Sew the sticks to the lollipop and ice-pop shapes. Sew a cone to each scoop of ice cream.
5. Cut out two 3½- and two 2½-inch squares for Jack's box. Sew a small square centered on a large square, to form two box shapes. Sew a spring shape to each box, a body shape to each spring, a head to each body, and a hat to each head.
6. Place every two constructed matching body shapes together. Tuck hands into their appropriate

places and pom poms into Jack's hat.

7. Sew the matching shapes together with a bit of **stuffing** between them.

8. Sew **yarn** hair to the doll's head.

9. Sew the dress shapes (follow dotted lines on the grid) together, and drape on the doll. Add a **gathered fabric or eyelet** apron.

10. Tie a length of **ribbon** into a bow around the bear's neck. Tie the doll's pigtails with **ribbons**.

1 square = ½ inch

Bears on a Trapeze, some Flying Angels, and a Barrel of Monkeys.

Little Miss Valentine and her Heart.

The Tooth Fairy, a Shaker of Salt, and the Easter Bunny.

Humpty Dumpty and the Learning Dollar.

King Neptune, the Mermaid, and
the Sea.

A Can of Soup, and Vegetables
in residence.

6

HOLIDAY CELEBRATIONS

Imagine a world without holidays—three hundred and sixty-five dawns and dusks yearly, with no people to honor, no events to commemorate, and no seasons to celebrate. But luckily there is a Christmas, a Chanukah, a Halloween, an Independence Day, a Valentine's Day, and many other days on the calendar that offer times for reflection, patriotism, family gatherings, and just plain fun. Children love holidays most of all, as they provide vacations from school, mornings to sleep late, and opportunities to learn about the people and historical milestones that make life so interesting and very worthwhile.

Little Miss Valentine

Send a special message of love via Little Miss Valentine.

The most worthwhile gift you can give or receive is one that originates from the heart. Such a present usually costs nothing, yet its value is priceless. Love is one of these intangible treasures, and Valentine's Day is its personal holiday. Here's a pretty heart with someone precious inside it—Little Miss Valentine. She is the official messenger of "I Love You" sentiments for the heart's young recipient. Remember, every day of the year can be Valentine's Day.

Heart

1. Cut two large same-size hearts from **red felt**. (The center height of the cut heart should be the length of a **standard-size zipper**.) Cut one in half top to bottom.

2. Sew the straight sides of the heart halves to the zipper.

3. Cut a smaller heart from **pink felt** and letters for a message from a **contrasting color of felt**.

4. Glue the message to the pink heart, and sew the pink heart to the zippered heart.

5. Place the two red hearts together, with **pre-gathered lace** tucked between them along the entire edge.

6. Sew the hearts together.

Little Miss Valentine

1. Miss Valentine is placed on a grid

(1 square = ½ inch). Enlarge the grid and the designs on paper to establish your patterns. Cut out the patterns.

2. Use the patterns to cut two body shapes from a **skin-tone felt**, two hair shapes from **red felt**, and two pinafore shapes from **white felt**. When cutting the back hair shape, eliminate the center opening.

3. Sew a front and back hair shape to each head of the body shapes.

4. Cut facial features from felt, and glue or sew them to the face.

5. Cut four shoe shapes from **red felt** and two small hearts from **pink felt**.

6. Sew a shoe to the bottom of each leg. Sew or glue the hearts to the shoes of the front body shape.

7. Place the doll shapes together, right sides facing out, and sew along all sides, leaving a bit of seam unsewn on one leg.

8. **Stuff** the doll and sew the open seam closed.

9. Sew the pinafore shapes together along the shoulders. Sew **ribbon** ties to the sides of each pinafore shape.

10. Cut out a **red felt** heart and a **white felt** pocket. Sew both in place on the front of the pinafore.

11. Slip the pinafore on the doll and tie in place.

12. Tie **ribbon** bows to the hair.

1 square = ½ inch

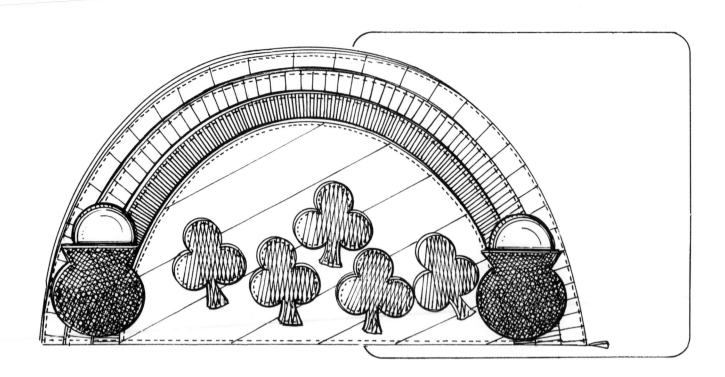

The Leprechaun's Pot of Gold for Saint Patrick's Day

At the end of this rainbow lies a pot o' fun.

Legend has it that at the end of any rainbow a pot of gold can be found. This colorful arc has a different tale: zipped up inside lives a lucky leprechaun who is anxious to share his good fortune with the rainbow's owner. The fun a youngster derives from this toy is well worth its weight in gold, especially when he or she finds a coin in each of the rainbow's pots, especially on Saint Patrick's Day.

Rainbow

1. Cut two semi-oval shapes 12 inches long and 7 inches high from **yellow felt**, for the base shapes of the rainbow.

2. Cut one **orange**, **red**, and **light blue felt** semi-oval from felt, each a little smaller than the preceding color, starting with the yellow base shape.

3. Cut out **green felt** shamrocks and sew them to the light blue semi-oval.

4. Sew the blue semi-oval centered on the red semi-oval, the red centered on the orange, and the orange centered on one yellow base shape. Make sure that all of the straight sides are flush with each other.

5. Cut two pots from **black felt** and sew one to each side of the rainbow, at the bottom. Leave the top, straight side of each pot unsewn.

6. Sew the straight sides of each base shape to a **12-inch zipper**. Sew the shapes together along the curved edge.

Leprechaun

1. The leprechaun is placed on a grid (1 square = ½ inch). Enlarge the grid and the designs on paper to establish your patterns. Cut out the patterns.

2. Use the patterns to cut two hats, hands, and pants and four shoes from shades of **green** and **brown felt**. Cut out one **orange felt** beard, a **pink** head shape, and a **black** pipe. The back head shape is the beard without the center opening. Cut it from red felt. The back of the jacket is made by cutting the two front jacket shapes as one piece.

3. Sew the beard to the face. Sew or glue on facial features.

4. Sew a hat to the top of the face and to the back head shape. Glue or sew a **yellow felt** buckle to the front hat shape.

5. Sew the back jacket to a pants shape. Sew the two front jacket shapes to the other pants shape, in line with the back jacket.

6. Sew a shoe to the bottom of each pants leg.

7. Sew the front head to the front body shape and the back head to the back body shape.

8. Place the two completed body shapes together, with a hand tucked into the arm seams.

9. Sew the two shapes together leaving a bit of seam unsewn.

10. **Stuff** the doll and sew the open seam closed.

11. Glue or sew the pipe to one hand.

1 square = ½ inch

The Easter Bunny Has a Surprise

This year the Easter Bunny is going all natural with a delivery of carrots and eggs.

Easter is traditionally a candy holiday, with baskets filled with jelly beans, marshmallow chicks, sugar eggs, and a chocolate bunny or two. Here's a delightful toy that will be the highlight of your youngster's candy basket. This bunny has gone the way of nature, delivering a special carrot and a decorated egg. It's for certain that it will be the first item your child reaches for as he or she forages through the jungle of candies and cellophane grass. This will surely surprise you and delight your dentist.

Easter Bunny and Carrot

1. The Easter Bunny and the carrot are placed on a grid (1 square = ½ inch). Enlarge the grid and the designs on paper to establish your patterns. Cut out the patterns.

2. Use the patterns to cut two bunny shapes and two carrot shapes from **appropriate colors of felt**. Also cut two egg shapes (3½-by-4½-inch ovals) from **white felt** and two carrot leaves from **green felt**.

3. Cut out felt facial features and ear middles. Sew or glue them to one bunny shape.

4. Place the two bunny shapes together and sew along all sides, leaving a bit of seam unsewn.

5. **Stuff** the bunny and sew the open seam closed.

6. Sew across the bunny's left arm, as indicated by the dotted lines on the grid.

7. Sew one half of a **large sewing snap** to each hand.

8. Place the carrot shapes together, with the leaves tucked between them at the top.

9. Sew the carrot shapes together with a bit of **stuffing** between them. Embroider carrot wrinkles.

10. Sew pretty **felt** designs on both egg shapes. Sew the shapes together, with a bit of stuffing between them.

11. Lay the carrot on the bunny, stretching it from one of the bunny's hands to the other. Fold the left hand over and mark where the bunny's snap halves touch the carrot. Do the same with the egg.

12. Sew corresponding **snap halves** to the carrot and the egg, where you have made the marks.

13. Snap on a carrot or an egg.

1 square = ½ inch

Stars and Stripes Pillow

Celebrate the Fourth of July with a Stars and Stripes commemorative pillow.

The Fourth of July is America's most celebrated holiday, commemorating the day the United States became an independent nation. This Stars and Stripes pillow can be a part of your youngsters' festivities, as the stars snap out for hours of glorious fun.

Stripes

1. Draw the shield on a 12-by-14-inch paper rectangle to establish your pattern. Cut out the pattern, then cut it in half horizontally.

2. Cut two top halves from **blue felt** and two bottom halves from **white felt**.

3. Sew each blue half to a white half to form two matching shield shapes. Sew three **sewing snap halves** to the right side of a blue half.

4. Cut three vertical stripes from **red felt** to fit equally spaced on the white half of a shield shape.

5. Cut out **white felt** eyes and sew or glue two to each red stripe, near the top. Embroider a smile on each stripe.

6. Sew the stripes, equally spaced, to the bottom half of one shield shape.

7. Place both shield shapes together and sew along all sides, leaving a bit of seam unsewn.

8. **Stuff** the shield firmly and sew the open seam closed.

Stars

9. Cut six stars, all the same size, from **white felt**. A star pattern can be traced from the Rocket Ship project (see page 59).

10. Cut out **blue felt** eyes and glue or sew two to three stars. Embroider smiles.

11. Sew each smiling star to a matching plain white star, with a bit of **stuffing** between them.

12. Sew corresponding **snap halves** to the backs of the stars, and snap the star in place.

A Trick-or-Treat Pumpkin With a Host of Faces

The face on this pumpkin bag changes to fit the treats.

Trick-or-treating can be quite rewarding, or the pickin's can be slim! Here's a trick-or-treat pumpkin sack that little ones will enjoy. The facial features are snapped into place. If a treat is healthy, a smile is snapped on; if it's unsatisfactory, a frown might appear.

Pumpkin

1. Cut two large, same-size pumpkin shapes from **orange felt**.

2. Sew vein lines, curved from top to bottom, on both pumpkin shapes for added strength.

3. Sew halves of **sewing snaps** to one pumpkin shape where the eyes, nose, and mouth fall. The mouth will require two snaps.

4. Cut a stem from **green felt** and sew it to the pumpkin shape with the snap halves.

5. Sew the two pumpkin shapes together along the bottom and sides, leaving the top third unsewn.

6. Sew a length of **heavy cord** to both sides of the pumpkin.

7. Cut assorted eyes, noses, and mouths, two for each shape, from **black felt**.

8. Sew each pair of matching shapes together.

9. Sew corresponding snap halves to the backs of the facial features.

10. Snap a face in place.

Pocahontas And Hiawatha Celebrate Thanksgiving in a Tepee

For the first time in history or legend, Pocahontas and Hiawatha are bosom buddies.

There was no chance in American history for Pocahontas and Hiawatha to ever meet: Pocahontas was the daughter of chief Powhatan, of Virginia, who lived in the early seventeenth century, and Hiawatha was a character made famous in a poem by Henry Wadsworth Longfellow. But thanks to the powers of imagination, these two young Indian friends come to life to share Thanksgiving dinner.

Tepee

1. From **light brown felt**, cut two triangles with a center height of 14½ inches and a 12-inch base. Cut one triangle in half vertically.

2. Sew the 14½-inch sides of the triangle halves to a **14-inch zipper**.

3. Cut out some Indian symbols from **assorted colors of felt**.

4. Sew symbols, scattered, on both triangles.

5. Place the two triangles together, and sew along the remaining sides.

Pocahontas And Hiawatha

1. Pocahontas and Hiawatha are placed on a grid (1 square = ½ inch). Enlarge the grid and the designs on paper to establish your patterns. Cut out the patterns.

2. Use the patterns to cut two body shapes from a **skin-tone felt** for each doll.

3. Cut eight shoes from **any color felt** and sew one to each foot of each doll shape.

4. Draw the front and back hair patterns on paper, following the design shown in the dotted lines on the body shape. The back hair does not have a center opening.

5. Cut out the patterns and use them to cut a back and a front **black felt** hair shape for each doll.

6. Sew a hair shape to each doll shape.

7. Cut out felt eyes and glue or sew two on each face from **appropriate colors of felt**. Embroider smiles. Sew a **ribbon** headband and a **feather** to the top of Pocahontas' face.

8. Place each set of matching body shapes together. Tuck a few feathers into the seam of Hiawatha's head.

9. Sew matching doll shapes together, leaving a bit of seam unsewn on each.

10. Stuff each doll and sew the open seams closed.

11. Cut two loincloth and two dress shapes from **beige felt**. Cut slits into the bottom edge of each shape.

12. Sew **ribbon or yarn** ties to the top corners of the skirt and dress shapes.

13. Tie the garments to their respective dolls.

1 square = ½ inch

Chanukah Fun with Candles and Gelt

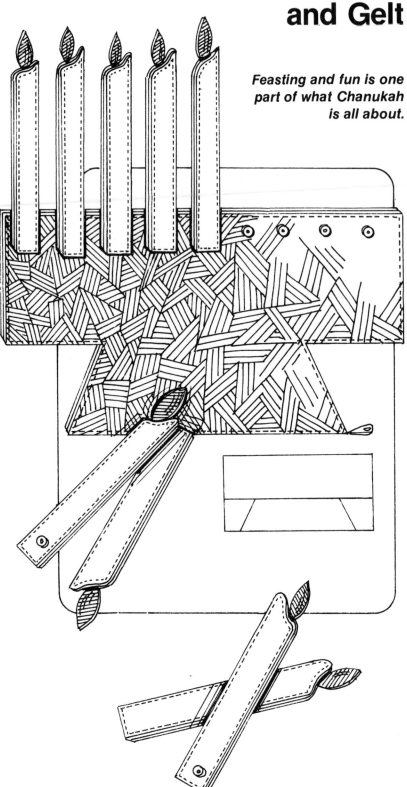

Feasting and fun is one part of what Chanukah is all about.

Chanukah, also known as the Festival of Lights, is an important holiday for the Jewish people. A candle is lit in the menorah every day of this special season, symbolizing the miracle that took place two thousand years ago, when one day's supply of oil burned in a temple lamp for eight days. Your little ones will enjoy the traditions and games of Chanukah, as they add a new candle to the menorah each day and spin the dreidel for gelt—money or some form of prize.

Menorah

1. Draw a menorah shape on a 7-by-13-inch paper rectangle. The base should be 8½ inches long. Cut out the pattern.

2. Use the pattern to cut two menorah shapes from **blue felt**.

3. Sew nine **sewing snap halves** along the top of one menorah shape, ¾ inch from the edge. Space them evenly.

4. Sew the base of each menorah shape to an **8-inch zipper**.

5. Sew the menorah shapes together along the remaining sides.

6. Cut eighteen ½-by-6-inch rectangles from **white felt** for the candles. Cut out nine **red felt** flames.

7. Place rectangles together in pairs, and trim the top width at an angle. Tuck a red flame between the rectangles at the trimmed end. Sew together with a bit of **stuffing** between each.

8. Sew the corresponding halves of the nine **snaps** to the candles, 1 inch from the bottom of each.

Dreidel and Gelt Game

1. Draw the dreidel shape on a 10-by-12-inch paper rectangle. The slanted side at the bottom point should be the measurement of a **standard-size zipper**. Cut out the pattern.

2. Use the pattern to cut two dreidel shapes from **white felt**.

3. Cut the paper dreidel pattern into four equal vertical sections.

4. Using the first and third pattern section, cut one of each shape from **blue felt**.

5. Sew the two blue shapes in their respective positions on the uncut dreidel shape.

6. Cut the four symbols, the Hebrew letters *Shin, Hay, Gimel,* and *Nun* shown in the drawing, from **brown felt**.

7. Sew the letters to the dreidel, one to each section.

8. Sew one bottom side of each dreidel shape to the **zipper**.

9. Sew the remaining sides of the dreidel shapes together with a **blue felt** rectangle tucked between the shapes at the top.

10. Cut dozens of **yellow felt circles** and sew pairs together. Use them as the playing gelt (money).

To Play the Game

Place the dreidel on a table or on the floor. Each player receives ten coins, or pieces of gelt. Each player puts one coin into the pot. The first player tosses a penny at the dreidel from a predetermined distance. If the coin does not land on the dreidel, the player tosses until one does land on it. When a coin lands on the dreidel in one of the sections, the following rules apply (from left to right): *Shin*, the player has to put one coin in the pot; *Hay*, the player takes half of the coins in the pot; *Gimel*, the player takes all the coins and a new game begins; *Nun*, the player receives nothing.

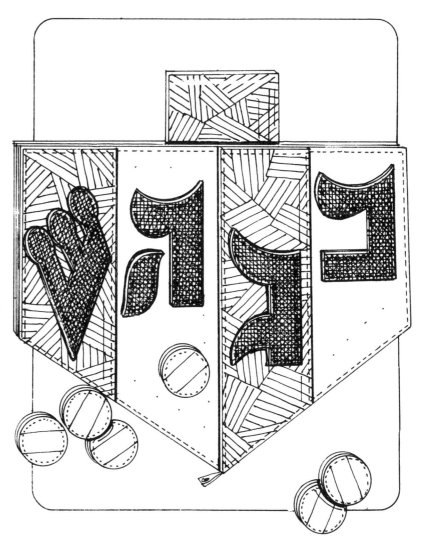

A Happy Clock for a New Year's Resolution

Here's a clock with a face that will either smile or frown for your children—all depending on them—on New Year's Day.

The first day of every new year is set aside for making resolutions which usually center around righting wrongs, changing bad habits, or approaching life with a new outlook. If you have children around your home, there are probably many aspects of their behavior you would like them to change. This adorable timepiece has a split personality. It smiles only when New Year's resolutions are placed in it. When the clock is empty or a promise is broken, it dons a disapproving frown. All you have to do is swivel the clock's mouth.

1. Cut two large circles from **white or a light-colored felt**.

2. Cut out felt eyes and sew them to one circle.

3. Cut out a red felt number twelve, in numerals, and sew it above the eyes.

4. For the clock's hands, cut four arrows, two long and two short, from felt.

5. Sew arrows together in pairs, with a bit of **stuffing** between them.

6. Center the hands on the circle with the face.

7. Tie one end of a length of sturdy thread to a large bead and knot in place. Thread the other end through a large needle.

8. Push the needle through the ends of the hands and through the center of the clock. Tie the end of the thread to another bead. The hands should move freely.

9. Cut two wide smiling mouths from **red felt**.

10. Sew the mouth shapes together with a bit of **stuffing** between them.

11. Sew one half of a **sewing snap** to the center of the mouth and the other half to the clockface, under the hands. Snap the mouth in place.

12. Place the two circles together and sew three quarters of the way around the edge, with two dark felt circles tucked between them at the bottom. The top should be open to hold your resolutions.

7

CHRISTMAS MAGIC

If every day of the year were Christmas, people would be continually friendly, generous, and peaceful; children would be perpetually filled with happiness, wonderment, and love. Since diversity makes the world go around, Santa Claus, lofty angels, and holiday feelings give rise to new seasons with different casts of characters. The pretty objects will eventually be packed away, but the spirit of this magical celebration can grow and glow in the hearts and actions of children of all ages every day of the year.

Here Comes Santa

a.

b.

c.

The Sleigh

1. The sleigh is placed on a grid (1 square = 1 inch). Enlarge the grid and the designs on paper to establish your patterns. Cut out the patterns.

2. Use the patterns to cut two sleigh sides and one back from **green felt**; and two runners from **yellow felt**.

3. Sew the sides to the back (the wide end of the back is at the top), along the 7-inch side.

4. Place the sides together, folding the back in half.

5. Sew the sides together along the bottom and front. You will have something that looks like a wedge of cheese, with no top.

6. Sew a runner to each side of the constructed sleigh.

Santa Claus

1. Santa is placed on a grid (1 square = ½ inch). Enlarge the grid and the designs on paper to establish your patterns. Cut out the patterns.

2. Use the patterns to cut two body shapes from **red felt**, four boots from **black felt**, one face from **pink felt**, one

Through rain, snow, or moonlit skies, Santa and his sleigh are on their way.

Santa Claus has a better track record for being on time than any postman in the world. No matter what the weather, jolly old Saint Nick manages to make his appointed deliveries. How he does it fascinates little children, who can never stay awake long enough to see him make his quiet entrance. This year Santa is a guest in your home, and lucky is the tot who finds the small Christmas treats in his sleigh.

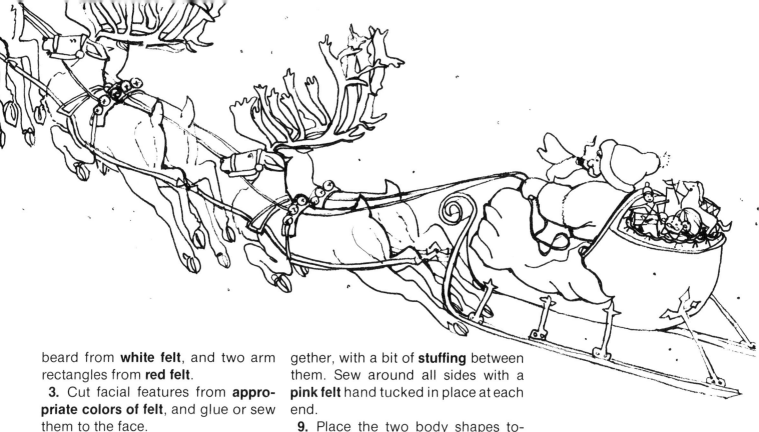

beard from **white felt**, and two arm rectangles from **red felt**.

3. Cut facial features from **appropriate colors of felt**, and glue or sew them to the face.

4. Sew the face to one body shape.

5. Sew the beard in place.

6. Sew a boot to the bottom of each leg of the two body shapes.

7. Cut narrow strips of **white felt** for the hat, arm, and boot trims. Sew each to its proper place.

8. Place the arm rectangles to-gether, with a bit of **stuffing** between them. Sew around all sides with a **pink felt** hand tucked in place at each end.

9. Place the two body shapes to-gether, with the constructed arms be-tween them on a slight angle.

10. Sew the body shapes together, leaving a bit of seam unsewn.

11. Stuff Santa and sew the open seam closed.

12. Sew a **white felt** circle to the top of Santa's hat.

1 square = 1 inch

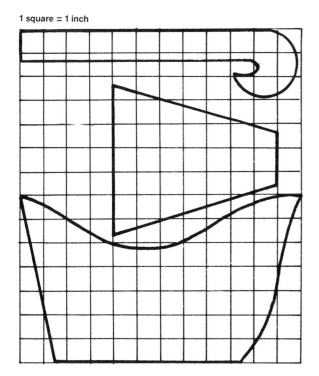

1 square = ½ inch

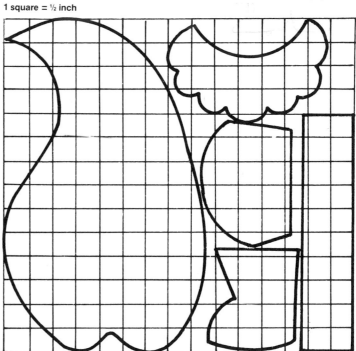

Holiday Treats That Sweeten a Plum Pudding

Your children will be playing with plum pudding treats, not just dreaming about them.

"While visions of sugar plums danced in their heads," reads the famous Christmas poem. But these adorable candies will have your little ones rocking and rolling for hours of fun. These popular treats include a peppermint stick, a piece of ribbon candy, and a peppermint swirl. And the all sweet goodies live in a plum pudding that is more than just a Christmas dream.

Plum Pudding

1. Draw a line across a 13-inch paper square, 3 inches from the top (see diagram). Draw a swirling peak centered on the line. Cut out for your pattern.

2. Use the pattern to cut two pudding shapes from **pink felt**.

3. Cut frosting designs from **white felt**.

4. Sew the designs to one pudding shape.

5. Sew the bottom of each pudding shape to one side of a **12-inch zipper**.

6. Sew the plum pudding shapes together along the remaining sides.

7. Cut a frosting swirl for the peak of

the plum pudding from **white felt**.
Sew in place.

Sugar Plum Treats

1. The patterns for the candy cane
and the ribbon candy can be traced
directly from the drawing. The cran-
berry and the peppermint-swirl
candy are 4-inch circles. The pop-
corn is a 4½-inch circle with a wavy
design cut into the edge.

2. Use the patterns to cut two of
each shape from **appropriate colors
of felt**.

3. For each treat, cut two eyes,
hands, and a mouth from **colors of
felt**.

4. Glue or sew two eyes and a
mouth to one shape of each treat.

5. Cut narrow stripes and swirls
from **red felt** for the candy cane and
the peppermint-swirl candy.

6. Sew the stripes and the swirls to
their appropriate shapes.

7. Sew matching shapes together,
with hands tucked in place. Leave a
bit of seam unsewn.

8. **Stuff** each treat and sew the open
seams closed.

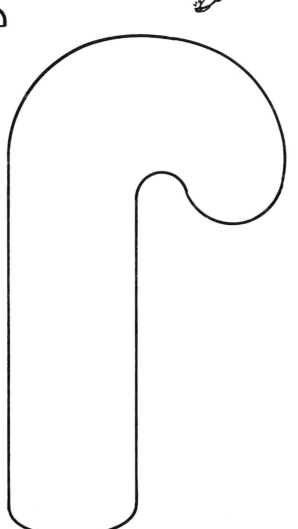

The Gingerbread Children Live in a Tasty House

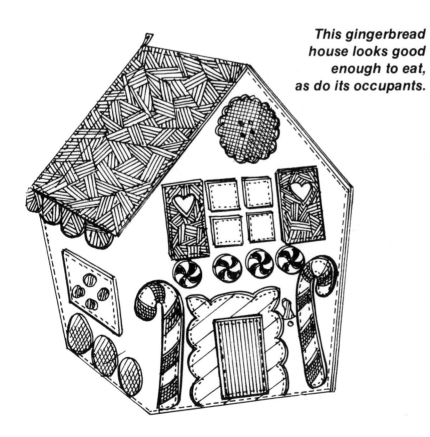

This gingerbread house looks good enough to eat, as do its occupants.

How lucky you would feel if you received a gingerbread house for Christmas. Every detail, from the window shutters to the roof shingles, would be marvelously crafted and colored, and your mouth would water for a bite all season long. Here's a gingerbread house that looks good enough to eat and contains two surprises, a gingerbread boy and girl. They live inside the house and are fun playmates not only during the Christmas season but throughout the year.

Gingerbread House

1. The gingerbread house is placed on a grid (1 square = 1 inch). Enlarge the grid and the designs on paper to establish your patterns. Cut out the patterns.

2. Use the patterns to cut two house

shapes from **light brown felt**.

3. Cut assorted candy and cookie details from **appropriate colors of felt** for the windows, door, shutters, and other details.

4. Cut a roof shape from **red felt**, along with some individual scalloped roof shingles.

5. Sew the roof and the shingles to one house shape.

6. Sew the appliqués to the house shape with the roof.

7. Sew the side of the roof of each house shape to one side of a **7-inch zipper**.

8. Sew the house shapes together along the remaining sides.

Gingerbread Children

1. The gingerbread figure is placed on a grid (1 square = ½ inch). Enlarge the grid and the design on paper to establish your pattern. Cut out the pattern.

2. Use the pattern to cut two body shapes for each doll from **light brown felt**.

3. Cut facial features from **appropriate colors of felt** and glue or sew them to one body shape of each doll.

4. Cut two simple pants and two skirts (with shoulder straps) from **colors of felt**. Also cut out a bib for each skirt.

5. Sew the pants and the skirts to their respective body shapes. Add a bow tie and buttons to the front boy body shape. Sew the bibs to the skirt shapes.

6. Place matching body shapes together and sew around all sides, with **white rickrack** tucked between them. Leave a bit of seam unsewn on each doll.

7. Stuff the dolls and sew the open seams closed.

8. Sew a **red and white felt** candy cane to one hand of each doll.

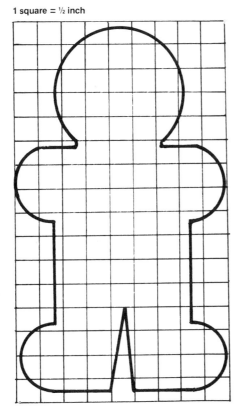

1 square = ½ inch

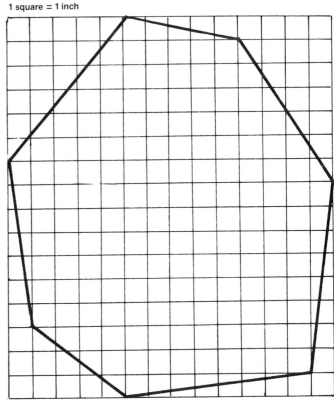

1 square = 1 inch

Madam Ginger and Her Nutcracker Brood

Madam Ginger may have nothing up her sleeves, but under her skirt can be found a brood of children.

One of the most interesting characters in the Nutcracker Suite is Madam Ginger. She gracefully dances about the stage wearing a dress with a bustly bottom. At a given musical cue, a brood of children make their entrances from under her skirt, a sight that never fails to delight children of all ages. With Madam Ginger in your home, this classical Christmas moment can be enacted time after time.

Madam Ginger

1. Madam Ginger's torso is placed on a grid (1 square = 1 inch). Enlarge the grid and the designs on paper to establish your patterns. Cut out the patterns.

2. Use the patterns to cut two head-and-arm shapes, two trunks, one front hair shape, and one back hair shape from **appropriate colors of felt**. Eliminate the center opening on the back hair shape.

3. The pattern for the skirt is a 13-by-20-inch rectangle with the top corners rounded and the bottom edge scalloped.

4. Use the skirt pattern to cut the back skirt shape from **colors of felt**. Cut the pattern in half, then cut both

front skirt-shape halves from felt, each in a different color.

5. Place the front skirt shapes on the back skirt shape, lining up all edges.

6. Sew the shapes together along all outer edges.

7. Punch holes into the scalloped edge of the skirt, or glue on felt circles.

8. Sew a hair shape to each head-and-arm shape. Sew or glue facial features to the front shape.

9. Sew the head-and-arm shapes together with a bit of **stuffing** between them.

10. Decorate each trunk shape with felt trim.

11. Pin the trunk shapes together, overlapping the trunk and skirt. Sew along all of the torso's sides, stitching all of the parts together. There should be an opening down the front of the skirt.

The Children

1. The pattern for the children can be traced directly from the drawing. Cut out the pattern.

2. Use the pattern to cut two body shapes for each doll from **skin-tone felt**.

3. Cut out facial features and hair for each doll from **appropriate colors of felt**. Glue or sew them on one of each pair of matching body shapes.

4. Cut out articles of clothing from **assorted colors of felt**.

5. Some clothing can be sewn directly to the body shapes before assembling the dolls, while others, such as skirts, can be added after the dolls are made.

6. Place matching doll shapes together in pairs and sew along all sides, leaving a bit of seam unsewn on each.

7. **Stuff** each doll and sew the open seams closed. Place the dolls in (under?) Madam Ginger's skirt.

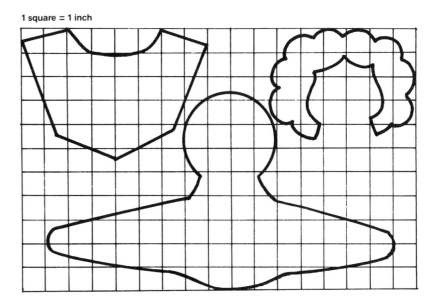

1 square = 1 inch

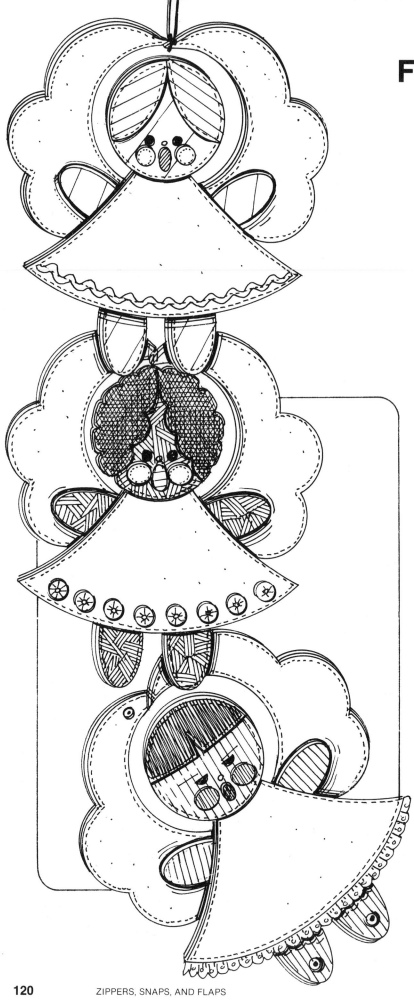

Flying Angels Bring Christmas Luck

Catch an angel, and good luck will be with you throughout the Christmas holiday.

Tradition has it that, like leprechauns, angels are bearers of good luck, if only you can catch one. Here is a troupe of angels that can be enjoyed individually as ornaments or hung on a wall when all snapped together. Your little ones are the recipients of good fortune this time, with so many precious friends to play with at Christmas.

Angels

1. The patterns for the angels are given in their actual sizes in the drawing. Trace them individually from the book onto tracing paper. Cut out the patterns.

2. Use the patterns to cut for each angel four wings and two skirts from **white felt**; two heads, four arms, and four feet from a **skin-tone felt**. Also cut a hair shape for both the front and back of the head.

3. Sew wing, arm, and feet shapes together in pairs, with a bit of **stuffing** between each.

4. Sew a smiling face and front hair shape to one head of each angel, and one back hair shape to its matching head shape.

5. Sew matching front and back head shapes to corresponding skirt shapes, one head shape to a skirt shape.

6. Sew **decorative trims or sequins** to the hemline of each skirt shape.

7. To assemble the angels, place matching body shapes together with the arms, feet, and wings tucked into

their appropriate places. The wings should overlap slightly at the top.

8. Sew the angels together along all sides, leaving a bit of seam unsewn on each.

9. Stuff the angels and sew the open seams closed. Now sew the overlapping wing tips together.

10. Sew **sewing snap halves** to the backs of the feet, and the corresponding halves to the tops of the wings, in line with each other.

11. Tie a **length of cord** to the overlapping wings of one angel.

12. Snap the angels together, and hang by the cord.

8

A SPECIAL PROJECT

The biggest toy of all, this really isn't a "toy" at all but rather an exercise to teach your children the importance of home. Anyone, or anything, should have a home of one's own. And here's one that's easy to build.

A Trunk to Hold Your Tot's Toys

A place for every toy, and every toy in its place . . . except at playtime.

Now that you have created a universe of toys for your little ones, it's time to create a permanent home for that universe. A toy trunk is the obvious answer, and here's one that can be made large enough to house all of the completed projects. Made of felt, it has no sharp edges and can be hung on a wall or tied to the foot of a bed. Now all that's left is to find a way to convince your children to place their toys in the trunk once the daily fun has ended.

Trunk

1. You will need two *very large* same-size **felt rectangles**. Make sure one long side equals the length of a large standard-size zipper.

2. Sew two **brown felt** strips and a lock with a keyhole to one rectangle.

3. Sew the top edges of both rectangles to a **large zipper**. (Or, for larger trunks, use two zippers. The zipper pulls should meet at the center.)

4. Sew the remaining sides of the rectangles together.

5. To hang the trunk on a wall, cut slits into the back of the trunk, evenly spaced and slightly beneath from the zippered side. Slip a **curtain rod** in and out of the slits, and attach the trunk to a wall.

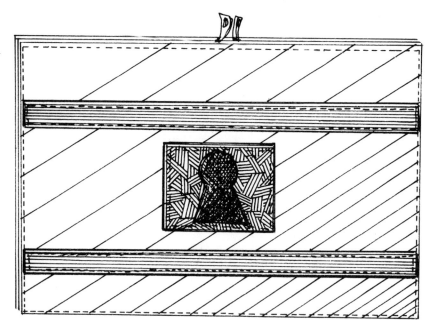

Grids

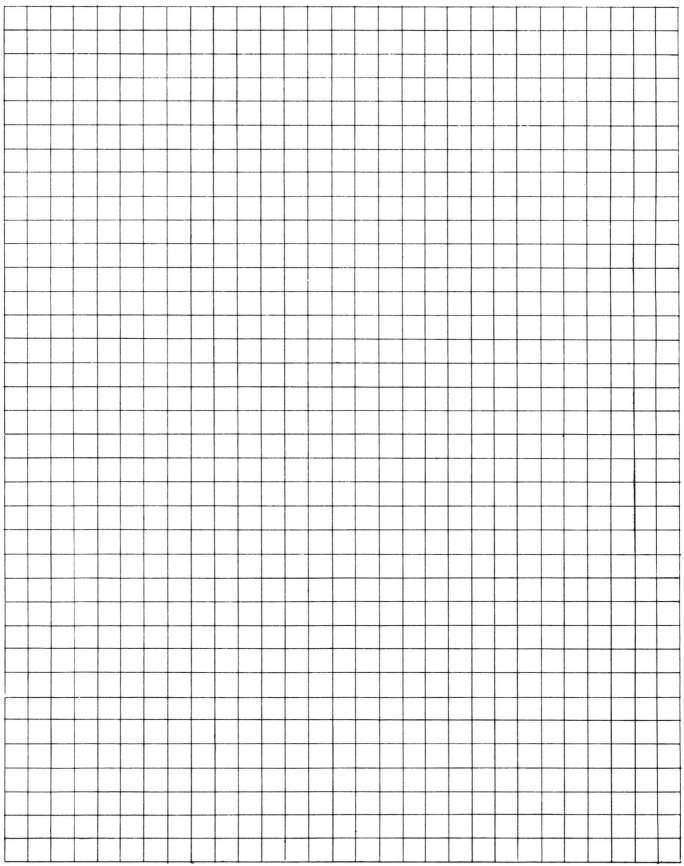

1 square = ¼ inch

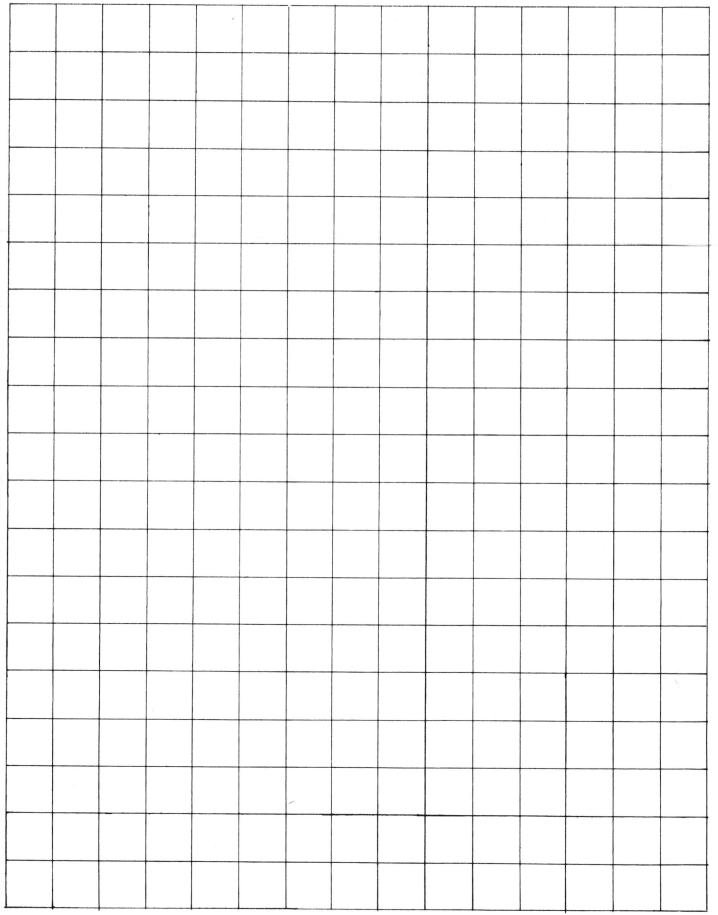

1 square = ½ inch

1 square = ¾ inch

1 square = 1 inch

Index